W9-AOE-562

SLAVERY IN THE AMERICAS

Life under Slavery

Deborah H. DeFord

Philip Schwarz, Ph.D., *General Editor*

CHELSEA HOUSE
PUBLISHERS
An imprint of Infobase Publishing

Slavery in the Americas: *Life under Slavery*

Chelsea House
An imprint of Infobase Publishing
132 West 31st Street
New York NY 10001

Library of Congress Cataloging-in-Publication Data
DeFord, Deborah H.
    Life under slavery / Deborah H. DeFord.
            p. cm. — (Slavery in the Americas)
    Includes bibliographical references and index.
    ISBN: 0-8160-6135-1 (alk. paper)
1. Slaves — United States — Social conditions — Juvenile literature. 2. Slavery — United States — History
    — Juvenile literature. 3.   Slave trade — United States — History — Juvenile literature.
    4.   African Americans — History — to 1863 — Juvenile literature. 5.   Plantation life — United States —
    History — Juvenile literature.   I. Title. II. Series.
    E443.D44 2006
    306.3'620973 — dc22

                                                                                    2005034651

Chelsea House books are available at special discounts when purchased in bulk quantities for businesses, associations, institutions, or sales promotions. Please call our Special Sales Department in New York at (212) 967-8800 or (800) 322-8755.

You can find Chelsea House on the World Wide Web at http://www.chelseahouse.com

Cover design by Smart Graphics
A Creative Media Applications Production
Interior design: Fabia Wargin & Luís Leon
Editor: Matt Levine
Copy editor: Laurie Lieb
Proofreader: Tania Bissell
Photo researcher: Jennifer Bright

Photo Credits:
The Bridgeman Art Library pages: title page, 19, 32, 41, 43, 79, 89, 105; The Granger Collection pages: 5, 31, 36, 77; Associated Press page: 10; New York Public Library, Astor, Lenox and Tilden Foundations pages: 14, 27, 53, 57, 67, 75, 81, 83; Library of Congress pages: 17, 49, 58, 63, 91, 93, 96, 104; Northwind Pictures Archives pages: 45, 99, 106; Photo History page : 65

Printed in the United States of America

VB PKG 10 9 8 7 6 5 4 3 2 1

This book is printed on acid-free paper.

PREVIOUS PAGE:

A slave family waits at a slave market about 1850. Despite difficult conditions,
American slaves developed strong family ties and unique traditions.

Contents

Preface to the Series

Philip Schwarz, Ph.D., *General Editor*

In order to understand American history, it is essential to know that for nearly two centuries, Americans in the 13 colonies and then in the United States bought imported Africans and kept them and their descendants in bondage. In his second inaugural address in March 1865, President Abraham Lincoln mentioned the "250 years of unrequited toil" that slaves had endured in America. Slavery lasted so long and controlled so many people's lives that it may seem impossible to comprehend the phenomenon and to know the people involved. Yet it is extremely difficult to grasp many aspects of life in today's United States without learning about slavery's role in the lives and development of the American people.

Slavery probably existed before history began to be recorded, but the first known dates of slavery are about 1600 B.C. in Greece and as early as 2700 B.C. in Mesopotamia (present-day Iraq). Although there are institutions that resemble slavery in some modern societies, slavery in its actual sense is illegal everywhere. Yet historical slavery still affects today's free societies.

Numerous ancient and modern slave societies were based on chattel slavery—the legal ownership of human beings, not just their labor. The Bible's Old and New Testaments, as well as other ancient historical documents, describe enslaved people. Throughout history, there were slaves in African, Middle Eastern, South Asian, and East Asian societies, as well as in the Americas—and of course, there were slaves in European countries. (One origin of the word *slave* is the medieval Latin *sclavus,* which not only means "slave" but also "Slav." The Slavs were people of eastern Europe who were conquered in the 800s and often sold as slaves.)

This drawing shows slaves carrying their master in a garden in ancient Rome. Slaves were a part of many societies from ancient times until the mid-1800s.

People found as many excuses or justifications for enslaving other people as there were slaveholding societies. Members of one ethnic group claimed that cultural differences justified enslaving people of another group. People with long histories of conflict with other groups might conclude that those other people were inferior in some cultural way. Citizens of ancient Greece and Rome, among others, claimed they could hold other people in bondage because these people were "barbarians" or prisoners of war. Racism played a major part in European decisions to enslave Africans. European colonists in the Americas commonly argued that Africans and their descendants were naturally inferior to Europeans, so it was morally acceptable to enslave them.

New World slavery deeply affected both Africa and the Americas. African society changed dramatically when the Atlantic slave trade began to carry so many Africans away. Some African societies were weakened by the regular buying or kidnapping of valued community members.

Western Hemisphere societies also underwent extraordinary changes when slavery of Africans was established there. Black slavery in North America was part of society from the earliest colonial settlements until the end of the U.S. Civil War. Many people consider the sale of about 20 Africans in Jamestown, Virginia, in 1619 the beginning of African slavery in what became the United States. American Indians and, later, Africans also were enslaved in Spanish colonies such as today's Florida and California and the islands of the Caribbean.

In early to mid-17th-century colonial North America, slavery developed slowly, beginning in Maryland and Virginia and spreading to the Carolinas in the 1670s. Southern colonists originally relied on white European servants. However, many of these servants had signed contracts to work only for a certain number of years, often to pay for their passage to North America. They became free when these contracts expired. Other servants rebelled or escaped. When fewer Europeans were available as servants, the servants' prices rose. The colonists hoped to find a more easily controlled and cheaper labor supply. European slave traders captured and imported more Africans, and slave prices dropped.

Soon, American plantations became strong markets for enslaved Africans. Tobacco plantation owners in the colonies around Chesapeake Bay—Maryland, Virginia, and North Carolina—and rice growers in South Carolina pressured slave traders to supply more slaves. In time, more and more slaves were kidnapped from their homes in Africa and taken to the colonies in chains to cultivate crops on the growing number of Southern plantations. Slaves were also taken to the Northern colonies to be farm workers, household servants, and artisans. In 1790, the U.S. enslaved population was less than 700,000. By 1860, it had risen to 3,953,750.

Similar circumstances transformed the Caribbean and South American societies and economies into plantation economies. There was a high demand for sugar in Europe, so British, French, Spanish, Portuguese, and other European colonists tried to fill that need. Brazil, a Portuguese colony, also became a thriving coffee-producing region. As the sugar and coffee planters became successful, they increased the size of their plantations and therefore needed more slaves to do the work. By 1790, Brazil was the largest American colonial slave society—that is, a society whose economy and social structure were grounded in slavery. Some 1,442,800 enslaved people lived in Brazil in 1790—twice the number that lived in the United States. Brazil's slave population grew slowly, however; in 1860, it was still only about 1,715,000. However, South American slaves were forced to work extremely hard in the tropical heat. The death rate of Caribbean and South American plantation workers was much higher than that of the North American slaves. Occasionally, a North American slave owner would threaten to sell unruly slaves to the West Indies or South America. Enslaved people took the threat seriously because the West Indies' bad reputation was widespread.

If the 1619 "first Africans" were slaves—the record is not completely clear—then there was a massive increase of the enslaved North American population from 20 or so people to nearly 4 million. In 1860, known descendants of Africans, both enslaved and free, numbered approximately 4.5 million, or about 14 percent of the U.S. population.

Slaveholders thought several numbers best measured their social, political, and economic status. These were the number of human beings they owned, the money and labor value of those people, and the proportion of slaveholders' total investment in human beings. By the 1800s, Southern slaveholders usually held two-thirds of

It is estimated that at least 11.8 million people were captured and shipped from Africa to the Americas. Many died during the slave ship voyage across the Atlantic Ocean. About 10 million survived and were sold in the Americas from 1519 to 1867. Nearly one-third of those people went to Brazil, while only about 3.8 percent (391,000) came to North America.

their worth in human property. The largest slave owners were normally the wealthiest people in their area. For example, one Virginian colonist, Robert "King" Carter, who died in 1733, owned 734 slaves.

Consider what it took for slavery to begin in North America and to last all the way to 1865 in the South. This historical phenomenon did not "just occur." Both slave owning and enslaved people made many decisions concerning enslavement.

Should people hold other people in lifetime bondage? Could Africans be imported without damaging American colonial societies? Should colonists give up slavery? It took many years before Americans reached consensus on these subjects. White people's consensus in the North eventually led to the outlawing of slavery there. The Southern white consensus was clearly proslavery. Enslaved peoples had to make different decisions. Should slaves resist slavery individually or in groups? Should they raise families when their children were likely to live and die in bondage? Over the two centuries in which North American slavery existed, enslaved people changed their opinions concerning these questions.

Some white colonists initially tried to own Indian slaves. However, because the Indians knew the local environment, they could escape somewhat easily, especially because their free relatives and friends would try to protect them. Also, European diseases simply killed many of these Indians. Once European enslavement of American Indians died out in the 18th century, Africans and their African-American descendants were the only slaves in America. The Africans and their children were people with a history. They represented numerous African societies from West Africa to Madagascar in the western Indian Ocean. They endured and survived, creating their own American history.

When Africans began families in North America, they created a new genealogy and new traditions regarding how to survive as slaves. They agonized over such matters as violent, or even group, resistance—if it was unlikely to succeed, why try? By the 1800s, they endured family losses to the interstate slave trade. Black families suffered new separations that often were as wrenching as those caused by the journey from Africa. Large numbers of black Americans were forced to move from the older (Upper South) states to the newer (Deep South) territories and states. They were often ripped from their families and everything they knew and forced to live and work in faraway places.

This undated illustration of pre–Civil War life depicts African men being held in slave pens in Washington, D.C., about 1850.

There was only so much that African-American people could do to resist enslavement once it became well established in America. People sometimes ask why slaves did not try to end their bondage by revolting. Some did, but they rarely succeeded in freeing themselves. Most individual "revolts"— more accurately termed resistance—were very localized and were more likely to succeed than large-scale revolts. A man or woman might refuse to do what owners wanted, take the punishment, and find another way to resist. Some were so effective in day-to-day resistance that they can be called successful. Others failed and then decided that they had to try to find ways to survive slavery and enjoy some aspects of life. Those who escaped as "fugitives," temporarily or permanently, were the most successful resisters. Frederick Douglass and Harriet Tubman are the most famous escapees. Solomon Northup was unique: He was born free, then kidnapped and sold into slavery. Northup escaped and published his story.

Although inhumane and designed to benefit slave owners, slavery was a very "human" institution. That is, slaveholders and enslaved people interacted in many different ways. The stories of individuals reveal this frequently complex human interaction.

There were, for example, in all the Southern states, free African Americans who became slave owners. They protected their own family members from slavery, but owned other human beings for profit. One such black slave owner, William Johnson of Mississippi, controlled his human property using the same techniques, both mild and harsh, as did white slave owners. Robert Lumpkin, a slave trader from Richmond, Virginia, sold thousands of human beings to

Deep South buyers. Yet Lumpkin had a formerly enslaved wife to whom he willed all his Virginia, Alabama, and Pennsylvania property in 1866. Lumpkin sent their children to Massachusetts and Pennsylvania for their education and protection. He also freed other slaves before 1865. How could men such as these justify protecting their own families, but at the same time separating so many other families?

The Thirteenth Amendment ended slavery in the United States. However, former slaves were often kept from owning property and did not share the same rights as white Americans. Racist laws and practices kept the status of black Americans low. Even though slavery ended well over a century ago, the descendants of slave owners and of slaves are still generally on markedly different economic levels from each other.

The Civil War and Reconstruction created massive upheaval in Southern slave and free black communities. In addition, slave owners were often devastated. African Americans were "free at last," but their freedom was not guaranteed. A century passed before their legal rights were effectively protected and their political participation expanded. The Reverend Martin Luther King's "I have a dream" speech placed the struggle in historical context: He said he had a dream that "the sons of former slaves and the sons of former slave owners will be able to sit down together at the table of brotherhood." (Today, he would surely mention daughters as well.) The weight of history had already delayed that dream's coming to pass and can still do so. Knowing the history of slavery and emancipation will help fulfill the dream.

Introduction

During the era of the slave trade, many slaves continued to follow their African traditions, as well as adopting new ones, creating a unique African-American culture in the process.

The first African slaves to land on the shores of the Americas came from many different nations. They were Ashanti, Twi, Zulu, Ibo, Yoruba, Ethiopian, Kumba, and others. When slave traders tore them from their old lives, the Africans did not lose their memories of home. They remembered the music and dances of home, as well as the foods, rituals, stories, political systems, and customs. Fearing that the slaves would rebel against their harsh life of forced labor, slaveholders often broke up groups of Africans from the same villages or tribes to make it more difficult for the captives to communicate with each other. Before long, the Africans began to lose their tribal identities.

When the Africans were carried away from their homes and deprived of their natural associations, they held on to the past in whatever ways they could. Then they found ways to weave old ideas into the pattern of their new lives. The result was an African-American culture that allowed the people to be themselves, despite the enslavement inflicted on them.

A band of musicians of the Yoruba people from western Africa is shown playing traditional instruments in this illustration from the 1800s.

African-American culture changed over time and from place to place. African Americans, like the Europeans who brought them to the New World, faced a variety of circumstances. Religion played an important role in the experiences of enslaved African Americans. Some lived in the Roman Catholic world of the Spanish, French, and Portuguese colonists. The Catholic Church actively encouraged slaves to convert and be baptized into Catholicism. Living and working on plantations owned by the church, slaves might have legal, church-approved marriages and baptize their children.

Other African Americans lived in the Protestant colonies belonging to Great Britain and the Netherlands. The Protestants encouraged the slaves to convert to Christianity but often did not consider them equal in God's sight. Protestant slaveholders rarely allowed their slaves to marry legally. This meant that in the eyes of the slaveholders, the marriages that African Americans made for themselves did not exist.

Despite the differences, African Americans all learned to speak the languages of their enslavers, while retaining elements of African languages that enabled them to speak a new, shared dialect of their own. They found ways to conduct their own religious services, use African remedies for illness and injury, and learn to read and write. They made families in spite of the frequent buying and selling of family members. They created music, developed their own holidays, and passed along wisdom in the form of folk tales and fables.

As Europeans colonized more and more of the Americas, they took slave populations with them. The African Americans in turn carried their culture into the new areas they helped to settle, from the islands of the Caribbean to Mexico, South America, and the vast North American continent. A single, distinct African-American culture developed, with regional variations, in what would become the United States.

THE GIFTS OF A CULTURE

In relation to the total population of North America, the African Americans came in greater numbers than any other immigrant group. They also came against their will. These factors contributed to their need for a common culture that continued from one generation to the next, holding them together with a strong identity of their own.

Despite centuries of white people treating them as property or beasts of burden, African-American culture allowed slaves to maintain a sense of their dignity as human beings. They supported each other and gained strength when their lives seemed unbearably harsh. They learned to find opportunities in their quiet moments to laugh, love, celebrate, and play. African-American culture also gave African Americans the courage to seek freedom and the abolition of slavery. Throughout the generations of slavery, African Americans maintained ideals that kept hope alive and gave them the strength to fight for freedom. In the process of building a culture that would sustain them in slavery, African Americans created a rich legacy that remains an important part of life in the Americas today.

In the United States and the other nations of the Americas, African Americans continue to identify with a common ancestry and shared heritage. At the same time, they take on greater and stronger roles as the fully acknowledged citizens they have become. Theirs is a story of survival, endurance, and courage that is told in their lives, literature, art, political advancements, and accomplishments.

The story of African culture under slavery in the Americas, and the part it played in the lives of the original enslaved Africans and their descendants, begins in 1502, when the first slaves arrived in Hispaniola (present-day Dominican Republic and Haiti). It continues to 1888, when Brazil became the last American nation to abolish slavery. It resonates beyond the final days of slavery and into the present, serving as a tragic reminder of wrongs in the past and the need for a better present and future.

1

Stolen People, Stolen Lives

Explorer Christopher Columbus stands before the king and queen of Spain after returning from his first voyage to the Caribbean. Columbus captured native people from the Americas and brought them back to Europe with him.

ARRIVAL IN THE AMERICAS

In 1492, Christopher Columbus, an explorer commissioned by Spain's government, became the first known European to arrive on a Caribbean island. He called the group of islands he discovered the "Indies," thinking he had found the Spice Islands of Asia (present-day Indonesia) by a new route.

People already lived on the islands of the Caribbean at the time of Columbus's arrival. Arawak Indians swam out to meet the first European ships that arrived in their waters. As the Europeans came ashore, the Arawak offered them food, water, and gifts. In his journal, Columbus reported that "they willingly traded everything they owned." He responded to their hospitality and generosity with violence. He wrote, "As soon as I arrived in the Indies . . . I took some of the natives by force in order that they might learn and might give me information on whatever there is in these parts."

Columbus was searching for sources of wealth, especially gold, for Spain. The Spanish government intended to conquer any lands that would make Spain richer. Columbus arrived with a conqueror's attitude about the people, as well as the land. As he wrote, "They [the Indians] would make fine servants. . . . With fifty men we could subjugate them all and make them do whatever we want."

Columbus's exploration party included Africans. Although they did not know it, they would be the first of a huge number of Africans to come to the Caribbean. These first few were free people. Most of the others arriving over the next several hundred years would be enslaved.

Christopher Columbus is shown meeting American Indians for the first time on the island of Hispaniola in this engraving from 1886.

Spain soon realized that Columbus had been mistaken about where he had landed. The Spanish government renamed the islands the West Indies. News of the "New World" spread, and other European nations soon sent their own explorers and colonists across the Atlantic. Where there were lands to claim, after all, there might also be gold, silver, diamonds, and exotic spices.

Spain established the first permanent European settlement in 1496 on the island named Hispaniola. Within 50 years, the Portuguese, British, French, Danish, and Dutch had established settlements on neighboring islands and on the mainland of Latin America. Although some gold was discovered, the real wealth of the islands would develop from plantations on which planters grew sugar, coffee, cotton, tobacco, and cacao (the bean from which cocoa is produced). As Columbus had suggested, the Europeans enslaved the native peoples "to make them do whatever" the Europeans wanted.

Most important to the newcomers was the work of the plantations. The European colonists forced the Indians to clear land and plant, tend, and harvest cash crops. The Europeans also made the Indians operate sugar mills, keep livestock, grow food to supply the plantations, and work as house servants.

However, the Europeans carried diseases that the Indians could not withstand. In addition, the Indians were poorly suited to the brutal working conditions imposed by the Europeans. Though some were able to escape their bondage, overall, the native population rapidly declined as the Indians died of illnesses and hardship. When the Europeans found themselves in need of more workers for their plantations, they turned to the slave trade, which had already been established between Africa and Europe. The New World would become a new market for buying and selling African people and their lives.

AFRICAN SLAVES COME TO THE NEW WORLD

The European slave trade of the New World began in 1502 in Hispaniola. Spain soon established settlements in Jamaica, Cuba, Puerto Rico, and Trinidad. In 1543, the Portuguese landed in Bermuda. Soon after, the French discovered Anguilla, the English laid claims to the Cayman Islands and St. Lucia, and the Dutch set up a stronghold on Curaçao.

European settlement spread to all the Caribbean islands, and with it slavery.

Spanish and Portuguese explorers were arriving at the same time in Central and South America. They established colonies in Mexico, Venezuela, Peru, Bolivia, and Brazil. Just as in the Caribbean, they forced the local Indians into labor and killed them with European diseases. By 1600, Mexico, Peru, and Brazil had become the three largest slave-holding societies.

The Caribbean Colonies of Europe

The imperial powers of Europe fought bitterly over control of the Caribbean. The islands lay along crucial trade routes. They also offered a tropical climate and fertile soil that was ideal for growing crops that were much in demand. Whoever controlled the Caribbean islands controlled a vast empire of trade.

The European governments imported millions of slaves into the Caribbean. They also brought hundreds of thousands of indentured servants (people who agreed to work for a master for a specific number of years) from Asia. Over time, many indentured Europeans arrived as well. All of these people, along with native peoples of the region, contributed elements of their ideas and lifestyles to the colonies of the Caribbean and Latin America. As a result, the region remains today a complex and multi-ethnic mix of people and customs.

At first, the African slaves arrived in relatively small numbers, meaning that the white population outnumbered them. Yet by 1620, approximately 300,000 Africans had arrived in the New World, and the balance between white and black shifted. At that time, a probable 80,000 African slaves had gone to Mexico. Another 80,000 to 90,000 had been sent to the Caribbean islands and other, mainland colonies. Brazil, the largest of all the colonies, had received about 130,000.

Only a handful of Africans stepped onto American soil north of Mexico and the Caribbean in the 1500s. When they did, it was usually in the company of early Spanish explorers, in Florida and in the Southwest. In the early years of the 1600s, the English and Dutch brought small numbers of slaves to settlements along the Atlantic coast of North America. Not until later in the century would slavery become a significant part of North American life.

European countries established colonies in these Caribbean and South American countries during the 16th century.

Wherever European colonists settled with slaves, they established slave laws that were meant to protect the white population and keep the enslaved people under control. Although slave laws differed from one place to another, they often included the same elements. Slaves could not carry weapons, gather in large groups, travel freely, or stay out after dark. Whites who beat or killed slaves received little or no punishment. In Puerto Rico, slaveholders tried to make it impossible for their slaves to escape and then claim to be free by branding the slaves' foreheads with burning hot metal. The branding permanently identified someone as a slave. (This practice continued until 1784.)

ISLAND WORK FOR AFRICAN-AMERICAN SLAVES

The first African slaves in the Caribbean were put to work at a variety of tasks. On the island of Hispaniola, for example, they mined gold and copper, but because little ore existed there, the mines soon closed down. On Martinique, slaves raised tobacco and cotton. On islands such as Jamaica and Cuba, slaves herded cattle, sheep, and pigs and grew such foods as plantains (similar to bananas) and maize (a kind of corn). On all the islands, slaves built houses for the slave owners and did household work.

The work that demanded the greatest amount of slave labor by far was on the sugar plantations, where slaves raised and processed the cash crop that Columbus had introduced in 1493. In the mid-1600s, the Dutch arrived in the Caribbean with the wealth and machinery to make sugar a major industry throughout the islands.

Barbados became the first island to be transformed by the sugar that traders called "brown gold." By 1680, Barbados alone was producing 8,000 tons (7,300 mt) of sugar a year on 350 sugar estates. With a population of 37,000, the African slaves now far outnumbered the 17,000 whites. By the end of the 1600s, Barbados contained more than 50,000 slaves. Between 1627 and 1807, 387,000 Africans would be taken to Barbados as slaves. Other islands tapped into the huge international sugar market as well.

The sugar plantations created a brutal, deadly world for the African slaves. They also caused much unease among the whites, who rightfully feared murderous uprisings of the blacks they kept in slavery. Black slaves often outnumbered the whites ten to one. The slaveholders' concern for their own safety led to even more hardships for the African Americans. The white people maintained control by terrorizing the slaves with dreadful punishments.

As the numbers of Africans increased in the Caribbean islands, the cultures of Europe and West Africa began to blend. Travelers to Barbados in the 1700s spoke of white people "lisping the language of the Negroes" and "adopting Negro style."

Many of the Europeans who owned plantations in the Caribbean lived in their home countries and hired overseers to manage the American Indian and African-American workers. The overseers had one major responsibility: to produce maximum crop yields for the owners. This meant driving the slaves to work inhuman hours, often without adequate rest or nourishment. As a result, many new slaves lived less than 10 years beyond the beginning of their labor on the plantations. This meant, of course, that the plantation owners needed a large supply of new slaves from Africa every year.

One priest describing the sugar work said that

slaves were generally awakened at four in the morning and worked until ten or eleven o'clock at night. Upon arising, the slaves went to the sugar mill where they ground eight, nine, or ten cauldrons of sugar. . . . At daybreak the sound of a bell summoned the slaves to take the sugar from the boiling house to the refinery and to put the "white sugar" in the sun to be dried. . . . When this work was completed, they returned to their homes for breakfast and to ready themselves for the fields.

The slaves worked up to 20 hours a day during harvest season. They had to fell trees with axes, then clear brush to make fields for the sugarcane. After harvesting the cane, they crushed it to extract the liquid it contained. Then came the boiling process that clarified the liquid and finally crystallized it into sugar.

After work, slaves returned to homes that provided poor sanitation and little comfort. In the 1500s and 1600s, many slaveholders expected their slaves to make their own housing. The Africans responded by building villages of huts made of straw and mud, constructed in a circle around a common area. Such villages mimicked the style of housing and community life the slaves had left behind in Africa.

Exhausted from their labors, the enslaved people had little time or energy left over for life away from their work. Yet when they were alone among their own, they learned to be defiant. They sang songs that mocked the masters and overseers. They learned to pretend they did not understand the white people in order to avoid more work or punishment. In such ways, they showed that they could not truly be "owned" and controlled.

LEARNING TO SURVIVE

In 1655, the British captured Jamaica from Spain and pushed the island firmly into what historians would call the sugar revolution. It soon became one of the largest and most brutal of the slave societies in the Caribbean. Here, as elsewhere, death rates for slaves exceeded birth rates. Three out of four babies of enslaved parents died before the age of five. New African slaves arrived every year from many tribes, including the Coromantee, Ibo, and Mandingo. The Coromantee were an especially proud and strong people. Before slavery was ended, they would lead many rebellions.

During times of rebellion, some slaves fought outright against the white people. Others chose secret ways to rebel. They poisoned the master, killed white babies, or destroyed property under cover of darkness. Many slaves escaped and formed hidden communities in the interior hills of the island. These fugitives were later called maroons.

The people of the maroon communities used the knowledge they had carried with them from Africa to survive off the land. Traditional medicine, based on herbal medicine used in West Africa, played a crucial role in their survival. They harvested wild lilies called aloe vera, which soothed burns and insect bites. The juice from the aloe leaves could be extracted and dried to produce an herbal medicine used to treat colds and constipation, as well as to purify a person's blood, eliminating elements that might cause disease.

The maroons prepared a tea from powdered cola nuts that relieved stomach pains and food poisoning. They collected oil nuts to extract the castor oil for use as a laxative— what they called a "cleanser" for the body. Annatto leaves were made into a tea used as a "worm killer" in children.

This illustration from a book published in 1910 shows what the maroon settlement of Trelawney Town in Jamaica might have looked like in the 17th century.

Maroons also prepared food in traditional African ways. After hunting and butchering wild pigs, the maroons heavily seasoned the pork with spices and salt, then wrapped it in leaves. The meat was cooked in a hole in the ground that had been filled with hot stones. This preparation is called "jerked" meat. (Various jerked meats have become popular today.) The maroons also grew vegetables and hunted other animals, such as pigeons and land crabs, for food.

WORDS OF WISDOM

The slaves who remained on the plantations in Jamaica commonly used proverbs to convey messages among themselves without letting the white people know what they were saying. For example, "Ant follow fat, fat drown ant" expressed the bad effects of greed. "Bad ting no hab owner" (literally, "a bad thing has no owner") meant that no one ever admits to a bad deed.

On the islands that were settled by Catholic nations, the slave owners and priests taught the slaves the beliefs and traditions of the Catholic Church. The slaves quickly found ways to blend these teachings with the beliefs and traditions of their African past. For example, they identified Catholic saints with the deities they had formerly worshipped in Africa.

One Catholic tradition, called Carnival, began as a recognition of Lent (it ends when Lent begins). Lent is the season leading up to Easter during which Catholics attend special religious services, and many do not eat meat. (The Italian word *carnevale* means "to put away the meat.") Carnival was celebrated as a costume party among the Europeans. Because the slaves were not invited, they made their own Carnival, adding ancient African traditions to those of the Europeans. For instance, they created parades using African drum rhythms, dancing their way around their villages in a circle that Africans believed would bring good luck. Carnival spread from island to island and continues to be celebrated today.

RELIGION IN THE SLAVE WORLD

In nearly every island slave community, the African Americans found ways to practice a religion that was their own. In Cuba, for example, most of the enslaved black people were Yoruba, from present-day southwestern Nigeria and eastern Benin. The Spanish slaveholders of Cuba forced their slaves to speak Spanish and worship according to Catholic traditions. In response, the Yoruba slaves banded together to retain their African religion.

Without the slaveholders' knowledge, the Yoruba slaves chose their own priests and gathered together in councils called *cabildos,* which were mutual-aid societies and social clubs. The Yoruba also created family units. These families, known as godfamilies or *ilé,* took the place of the traditional families that were routinely torn apart in the slave trade.

The Yoruba worshipped spirits they called *orisha.* They found that they could safely continue this practice by calling their *orisha* by the names of Catholic saints. Over time, Catholic practices merged with the African Americans' native beliefs to create a religion that was neither one nor the other, but rather both. This religion hidden within another religion came to be called Santería.

Dance and music filled a great part of the slaves' free time after work. Historians believe that many of the island and Latin American dance styles of today originated in Africa and were shaped by the slaves' lives. For example, the conga, which people dance in a snaking line, may have originated with slaves who were chained together in a line while they worked. To give themselves strength and courage to get through the drudgery of their work, they would sing or chant. When slavery ended, the freed African Americans continued the music and dance traditions that reflected the life they had lived under slavery.

A LASTING LEGACY

By the early 1700s, African Americans made up more than half the population of the Caribbean islands. The island cultures reflected the food, music, religions, and beliefs of the hundreds of African nations whose people had been kidnapped, sold, and enslaved.

The black slaves did more than any other group to create the industries of the islands. With their unpaid work, they made the white slaveholders rich. Whatever the slaves had, they had to fight to gain. They worked hard, suffered unimaginable hardships, and died young. Yet their determination to survive and maintain a culture meant that they made a lasting mark on the Caribbean islands. Their descendants and their influence continue to the present day.

2

Planting the New World

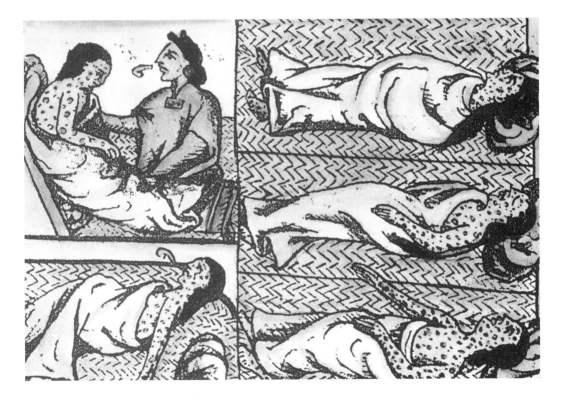

In addition to slavery, the Spanish brought a disease called smallpox to the New World. Thousands of Indians died as a result. This illustration from a 16th-century book shows Aztec devastated by the illness.

COLONIZATION CONTINUES

While European nations battled for control of the Caribbean, Spanish and Portuguese colonists were claiming parts of Central and South America for their nations and for the Roman Catholic Church. Spaniards and Portuguese went to the Americas in search of gold and silver. By the mid-1500s, they had found rich veins of these metals in the colonies of Mexico and Peru. As they did in the Caribbean, the colonists forced the Indians of these regions to labor in the mines. Just as in the Caribbean, the Indians fell ill of European diseases or died during the dangerous work of mining. Before long, Antonio de Mendoza, who ruled Mexico for Spain, wrote home to Spanish officials, begging for African slaves. "The silver mines are increasing, as each day more and more are discovered," he wrote, "while the [Indian] slaves continue to decrease."

Indian slaves are shown laying the foundation for a Spanish cathedral in Mexico City in 1522. Indians were forced to perform many backbreaking tasks for their European masters.

Slaves were already kept in Spain and Portugal before those nations sent colonists to the Americas, and both nations had already established slave laws. In part because of the influence of the church, the laws sought to limit mistreatment of the slaves by their owners. The laws also provided ways for slaves to protest when their rights were violated. In the New World, however, as the number of African slaves increased and eventually surpassed the white population, Spanish colonists created new, harsher laws to protect themselves from the people they enslaved.

MEXICO AND PERU

Many of the mining enterprises that developed in Mexico were isolated from Indian settlements. As a result, the majority of South and Central America's earliest African slaves went to Mexico. By 1570, Africans did nearly half of all the labor of the mines, both above and below ground.

Almost from the beginning, slaves sought to escape. Because parts of Mexico were mountainous and hard to reach, escaped slaves were able to form communities of fugitives, called *cimarron palenques* (maroon villages). The time would come when these villages formed the basis of large, free black communities. In the meantime, they provided a place where fugitive slaves could maintain many features of their African culture.

Slavery in Mexico reached its peak in the mid-1600s, then began to decline as the Mexican Indian population began to recover and grow. Over time, free laborers took the place of slaves.

Peru, like Mexico, depended heavily on slave labor at first. Close to 2,000 African slaves helped the Spanish conquer

Peru in the 1530s and 1540s. As the Spanish settled this new colony, the number of imported slaves grew, with many of them settling in the major city of Lima.

The African slaves of Peru worked a much wider variety of jobs than did those of Mexico. While some slaves were soon sent to the tropical lowlands, where gold had been discovered, many more labored to supply the cities with the necessities of life. Small families of slaves worked truck farms (cultivated fields called *chacras,* located on the city outskirts). They raised vegetable gardens and orchards and planted fields with grain. Along Peru's coast, meanwhile, individual sugar estates employed groups of 40 to 100 slaves. Slaves also worked in coastal vineyards and on plantations of mixed cash crops.

In the cities, many slaves learned skilled trades, such as metalworking, textile work, and construction. They also worked at less skilled jobs, such as fishing or food-handling and processing. The types of jobs done by slaves sometimes made it profitable to slaveholders to rent out their slaves to others.

As time passed in these colonies, as well as in what would become Colombia, Panama, Venezuela, and Argentina, slaves had a much better chance of buying their own freedom than they would have either in the Caribbean or on the North American continent. They could often retain some small part of the wages they earned when their owners rented them to others. The money they saved enabled them to purchase their freedom.

Although the Catholic Church did not condemn slavery, it did teach that the slaves were people who had souls, just as Europeans had. Therefore, Catholic slaveholders could not easily justify treating slaves as though they were animals.

Over time, Africans and Indians intermarried. Both groups also intermarried with the Spanish colonists. As these people produced children, the differences between them blurred. People's status (slave or free, Spanish-speaking or not) and economic class (laborer, landowner, or skilled craftsperson) became more important than the color of their skin.

Naming the Races

As races and nationalities intermixed, new classifications of racial identity developed. In addition, various names for the Africans in the Spanish colonies were created based on how long they or their families had been in the New World, where they were born, and how well they knew the language and culture of their owners. The following terms had great importance for both the slaves and the slaveholders. The names determined how people were treated and what jobs were open to them.

- A *mestizo* was a person of mixed Indian and Spanish ancestry.
- A *mulatto* was a person of mixed African and Spanish ancestry.
- A *zambo* was a person of mixed African and Indian ancestry.
- A *bozal* was an African slave newly arrived from Africa.
- A *ladino* was an African slave who had successfully picked up Spanish customs and culture.
- A *criollo* (creole) was a person of African descent born in the Americas.

AFRICAN SLAVES IN BRAZIL

Of all the colonies that relied on slave labor, none imported more enslaved Africans than Brazil did. The Portuguese first arrived in Brazil in 1500. Explorers took a special interest in the brazilwood that grew there. Natives of Brazil used the plant to produce red and purple dyes. These colors were much sought after in Europe and worth a lot of money. In 1530, the king of Portugal, João III, sent the first settlers to the land claimed by his nation. The colonists soon realized that Brazil also had the perfect environment for growing sugar.

The newcomers quickly turned to slavery for the workforce they needed to work sugar plantations and mills. Like the other Europeans, they first enslaved the American Indians. By the mid-1500s, though, they began importing large numbers of Africans.

Indians labor in a Spanish silver mine in this drawing by the explorer Samuel de Champlain from his book *Voyage to the West Indies and Mexico,* published about 1600.

By the early 1600s, Portugal's success in Brazil attracted the attention of the Dutch government. In May 1624, the Dutch captured the city of Salvador. From there, they went on to seize land both north and south. They hoped to capitalize on brazilwood and sugar. Like the Portuguese, the Dutch depended on African slave labor to accomplish their aims.

Life for slaves on sugar plantations in Brazil was as harsh as it was elsewhere. The average life span of slaves, once they began this work, was a mere eight years. Many slaves ran away, creating hidden communities called *quilombos*. The most famous of these, named Palmares, continued from the early 1600s to 1694. At its peak, its population totaled about 20,000.

THE ART OF SELF-DEFENSE

Many Brazilian slaves lived in slave quarters called *senzales*. These consisted of slave-constructed houses that were attached and laid out in an extended rectangle similar to a present-day barrack. The quarters were divided into separate units for unmarried men and families. Most slave marriages were not legally accepted by the Brazilian authorities. Even so, the slaves formally sanctioned the free unions they created and lived in family groups that the slave community recognized and supported.

Within the slave quarters, the African Americans adapted their traditional ways to their new lives, maintaining a clear sense of themselves and their dignity as human beings. For example, Africans imported to Brazil from Angola are believed to have brought with them a martial art known as capoeira. This style of self-defense could be practiced in such a way that it looked like a traditional dance of Africa, combining music, dance, and acrobatics. The slaves would practice capoeira in the slave quarters after their work was done, and the slaveholders would have no idea that it was a martial art.

Palmares

The fugitive slaves of Palmares created a mini-nation of their own. They organized a government and grew crops, fished, and hunted to sustain themselves. They also traded illegally in gold with those who wanted to sidestep the laws of the Portuguese king.

Portuguese and Dutch colonists wanted to do away with the community that offered a safe haven to other runaways. The black leaders of Palmares, meanwhile, knew that their power depended on size. In order to increase their population, they actually stole slaves from surrounding plantations. These enslaved people could win freedom in Palmares by bringing in other captives. To further ensure their numbers, the Palmares leaders made it illegal to leave the community.

Palmares inspired slaves to resist their enslavement. Although the European Brazilians eventually succeeded in destroying the settlement in 1694, its legend continued, and the site continued to be remembered in song and dance in the celebration of Carnival.

In the sugar fields, slaves also practiced *maculele,* a warrior dance that originated in the Congo. Slaves used sticks or machetes, both tools of the sugar plantations, in this martial art. At the end of the harvest, slaves would face off as attacker and opponent. As other slaves created a rhythm of clapping and drums, the pair executed a variety of attack and defense moves.

THE SECRET LIVES OF SLAVES

African slaves in Brazil learned to adapt their various African tribal languages to the Portuguese language of the slaveholders and the native languages of Brazil. The resulting pidgin (a simplified form of mixed languages) became an easy way of communicating between cultures while still keeping bits and pieces of the African dialects alive.

In similar ways, African Americans combined their native religions with the Catholic practices of Portuguese Brazil. West Africans believed that worship involved direct communication with any one of a number of *orixa* (the Portuguese version of the Yoruba word *orisha*, meaning gods or saints). This idea was similar enough to the Catholic practice of praying to saints that the African slaves could combine the two, identifying their *orixa* with the Catholic saints (as the Cuban slaves did). The resulting combined religion of the Brazilian slaves is called Candomble.

Catholic leaders prohibited the music and dance of traditional African worship, so the slaves conducted their religious ceremonies as though they were parties. They held special holiday dances called *batuques*, in which participants were taught how to make and play drums, perform ancestral dance steps, and echo the rhythms of Africa. The

Muslim slaves from Africa were less likely to combine their religion with that of their enslavers. In fact, historians believe that some slave uprisings and rebellions in the 1800s were parts of a well-organized jihad (holy war), resisting "the enslavement of Allah's children by Christians."

rhythms, music, and dance that developed would later be known as the samba, a dance style that is still popular today. To people who practice Candomble, the word *samba* means to pray to one's personal *orixa*.

THE PERSISTENCE OF SLAVERY IN BRAZIL

In the second half of the 1600s, sugar production in the Caribbean islands began to dominate the European market, making Brazil's sugar plantations less profitable. By then, Brazil had imported half a million slaves to work on those plantations. By the 1690s, deposits of gold were found in Brazil, shifting the attention of European colonists to a new source of wealth. Within 30 years, diamonds were also discovered. Before the end of the 1700s, an additional 1.5 million African slaves had been imported to fill the labor needs of the gold and diamond mines.

Both gold and diamonds could be found in deposits on the banks and in the beds of rivers. Slaves were put to work with pans and waterworks that they used to wash the soil. For diamonds, slaves would dig canals to divert streams, then dig deep into the riverbeds. As they worked, overseers watched from backless seats designed to keep them alert as they checked that no precious stones were stolen. Slaves who found a diamond of a particularly large size (18 carats or more) were given their freedom.

Many slaves worked in food production, farming and ranching to supply the mining towns. The Africans were the only immigrants in the New World who had experience farming in tropical climates. Their knowledge made them especially good at raising crops, both for the slaveholders and for themselves.

The slaves' knowledge of plants and farming also kept their traditions of healing and magic alive. African-American elders (both women and men, usually unmarried) specialized in the medicinal and magical use of plants. They learned about the South American plants from enslaved Indians. These elders became a central part of a slave community, holding it together with the belief that their magic worked and could be trusted to operate for the good of the group.

Brazilian slaves toil in a sugar mill refining sugarcane in this illustration from 1835.

SLAVERY'S GROWTH

In the 1770s, Brazilian planters entered into a new cash-crop business—coffee beans. The coffee plant itself originated in Africa, as did the additional 1.5 million slaves Brazil would import to meet the needs of the coffee plantations. By 1800, Brazil had the largest slave population in the world.

Brazil would be the last country in the Western Hemisphere to abolish slavery. Both coffee growers and politicians fought against abolition. "Brazil is coffee," said one member of Brazil's government in 1880, "and coffee is the negro." Before Brazil finally abolished slavery in 1888, it had imported more than one-third of the total number of African slaves brought to the New World. Between 4 million and 5 million people were taken from their homes and lives to serve the greed of this New World nation. In exchange, they added a strong strain of African culture to the religions, foods, music, and languages of the region, enriching the world they were forced to inhabit.

3

Colonial Expansion in North America

This illustration depicts African slaves arriving in Jamestown, Virginia, in 1619. Slavery was practiced throughout the 13 British colonies, including those in the North.

SLAVES OF THE BRITISH

Slaves had been toiling in the Caribbean and Latin America for at least a century when British colonists of Jamestown, Virginia, purchased about 20 Africans from a Dutch slaver in 1619. These were the first Africans in British North America to be purchased as workers for the new settlement's tobacco plantation, although it is not completely clear whether the Africans were slaves or indentured servants. In 1626, the Dutch imported the first African slaves to their settlement of New Amsterdam (which would become New York City in 1664, when the British took possession of it). Connecticut followed in 1629, Maryland in 1634, and Massachusetts in 1641.

Eventually, every British colony in North America included enslaved African Americans. At first, slaves arrived a few at a time, usually from the West Indies. In cities, they worked on the docks or as servants in people's homes. Outside of the towns, they worked on farms, in tanneries (making leather), in mines, or at ironworks.

By the end of the 1600s, colonists in the Chesapeake region (Virginia, Maryland, and North Carolina) were beginning to make significant profits growing tobacco. Tobacco plantations needed workers. Indentured servants from Europe worked the plantations at first, but they owed colonial sponsors only a certain number of years' labor, and then they were freed. A slave was purchased for life, so plantation owners turned to slave traders to acquire their labor force.

As the numbers of slaves in the North American colonies increased, each colony passed its own slavery laws. The laws made slavery legal and stated that because slaves were property, not citizens, they could not own property or make legal contracts, including marriage contracts. They could not testify against white people in court or receive a trial with a jury. They could not carry weapons, leave a plantation without a pass, or defend themselves against white people.

As in every society with slaves, slave codes did not stop slaves from fighting against slavery. They might resist by poisoning slaveholders, stealing from them, damaging their tools, or setting their property on fire. In response, the whites in authority resorted to whipping rebellious slaves, hanging them, burning them at the stake, or disfiguring or branding them. People were fined for giving shelter to fugitive slaves, and if the runaway slaves were caught, they might be branded to show that they needed to be watched closely.

In this illustration, slaves on a 19th-century Southern cotton plantation discuss the possibility of escape.

As the plantation culture spread, particularly in the South, slave traders brought more black people directly from Africa. This created a class distinction among the slaves themselves. American-born slaves, like white slaveholders, referred to African-born blacks as "outlandish negroes" and treated them with disrespect. New African arrivals who could not speak English had an especially hard time. One African named Olaudah Equiano, who was captured in the mid-1700s, later described his experience. He wrote, "I was . . . exceedingly miserable, and thought myself worse off than any . . . of my companions; for they could talk to each other [in English], but I had no person to speak to that I could understand."

SLAVE LIFE IN THE NORTH

Since the North's climate did not support plantation crops, the slave population in the North was never as large as that in the South. Northern investors and merchants, however, became heavily involved in the slave trade. They built many of the ships used in the trade, and they bought and sold African lives and slave-produced goods for profit. In that way, slavery had a strong effect on the North, as well as the South.

In the North, most African-American slaves worked as domestic servants in people's homes and on farms, especially those of doctors, ministers, and wealthy merchants. The slaves also worked in various skilled trades and on the docks.

Although slaves' lives were harsh, no matter where they were enslaved, African Americans in the North generally received kinder treatment than they did on the plantations of the South. Their smaller numbers in the North made them less likely to rebel, which in turn made them less frightening to their owners. This meant that the slaveholders might feel less need to inflict constant punishment to keep the slaves in line. In addition, many Northern slaveholders considered it their duty to instruct their slaves in religion and good behavior.

In the mid-1700s, African Americans made up as much as 30 percent of the total population of some Northern townships, such as South Kingstown, Rhode Island—mostly on rural estates. Because the lives of Northern slaves did not include the brutal work of the plantation, they tended to live longer and more of their babies survived. With a higher concentration of African Americans in a smaller area, they were able to use their rare free moments to gather together and create a culture of their own.

'Lection Day

Slaves in Northern cities found various ways to make a culture that was their own. In Philadelphia, Pennsylvania, for example, slaves requested that the city give them a separate area in the city's Strangers' Burial Ground to bury their dead. They used the designated area as a gathering place on Sundays, holidays, and fair days, when many had no work.

Some slaves created a political world of their own as well. When white colonists celebrated election days, blacks enjoyed their own celebrations at which they elected their own kings and governors to settle disagreements among themselves. They also held 'Lection Day parades and shared food and music that recalled the traditions of Africa.

SLAVES IN THE TOBACCO SOUTH

Many white people in the South never owned slaves. Others, like slaveholders in the North, owned only two or three slaves who worked as domestic servants, alongside a master in a trade, or on the family farm. Only a small proportion of Southern slaveholders owned dozens or hundreds of slaves. These plantation owners grew cash crops such as tobacco, indigo, rice, cotton, and sugarcane.

In the Upper South, including Virginia, Maryland, and North Carolina, tobacco captured the interest of British colonists early on. American Indians had long been growing and smoking tobacco. The English settlers learned to smoke as well, then carried tobacco back to England, where it became hugely popular. Before long, tobacco came to be called "black gold" because of the wealth it brought to the people who cultivated and sold it.

Tobacco cultivation required many workers, and colonists soon found that the cheapest laborers were African-American slaves. Tobacco production took 11 months of every year from seed to harvest to packing. Beginning in late January, slaves would prepare the fields for planting, mend and ready tools, and start seeds in special beds. By March, they started transplanting the seedlings to the fields. Through the growing season, the plants needed constant care, shading from the hot summer sun, and loosening of the soil. At harvest, the tobacco leaves were cut, hung to dry, and then rolled for shipment to England.

No sooner would one year's work end than the slaves would have to prepare for the next year. Slaves were put to work in the tobacco fields when they were seven years old. When slaves were too old to work the fields, they took care of the babies and toddlers whose enslaved mothers worked in the fields.

This picture shows a slave cabin in Virginia that was typical of the living conditions for slaves in the South.

The work of the plantation left little time or privacy for the slaves who did the crop work. They carved what culture they could out of the precious free moments they had. The slaves typically lived in small, rough quarters with dirt floors and little or no furnishings. Each family might have a blanket, an iron pot for cooking over a fire, and a mill for grinding the corn they were given to eat. Their clothes were made of rough homespun wool or cotton. As one Maryland slave later explained, "We lived in rudely constructed log houses, one story in height, with huge stone chimneys, and slept on beds of straw. Slaves were pretty tired after their long day's work in the field. Sometimes we would, unbeknown to our master, assemble in a cabin and sing songs and spirituals."

Slave Sustenance

Slaveholders provided only the most basic food for their slaves. One slave from a tobacco plantation in Virginia recalled the food he and his fellow workers had in this way:

On Saturday, each slave was given 10 pounds [4.5 kg] of corn meal, a quart [0.9 l] of black strap [molasses], 6 pounds [2.7 kg] of fat back, 3 pounds [1.4 kg] of flour and vegetables, all of which were raised on the farm. All of the slaves hunted . . . or fished. . . . Each family was given 3 acres [1.2 ha] to raise their chickens or vegetables.

Historians believe that the slaves often cooked one-pot meals, such as vegetable stews seasoned with pork fat. The food could simmer all day over a low fire while the slaves labored. This method of cooking echoed the traditions of West African food preparation.

Because the slaveholders typically provided little variety of food for the African Americans to eat, slaves often grew small gardens of their own or hunted animals. Modern archaeologists have found broken shards of dishes and cooking pots that slaves formed out of the clay in the ground.

Archaeologists have also found pipes that the slaves must have used for smoking tobacco themselves. Many of these dishes and pipes look just like those found in Africa, with African decorations carved onto them.

The slaves feared discovery of whatever personal belongings they had brought with them or made themselves. Slaveholders considered everything on their plantations their own property. So slaves would sometimes dig cuddy holes, pits lined with boards under their floors, where they could store root vegetables they had grown—and also hide personal items out of sight of the plantation owners.

SLAVE MARKETS

By the mid-1700s, when the colonies were growing and plantations had become larger and more numerous, planters needed more slaves. Up to this point, most African slaves had been brought to the British colonies from the West Indies. Now slave traders resorted to bringing slaves directly from Africa. Instead of arriving a few at a time, whole shipments of slaves arrived. They were taken to port cities such as New Orleans, Louisiana; Charleston, South Carolina; and Philadelphia, Pennsylvania. There, slave traders set up markets where the slaves were auctioned off like cattle. Alongside the new arrivals were people who had already been enslaved but whose owners now wanted to sell them.

From about 1800 on, the markets became big business. When slaves arrived in a market city, they were taken to pens or cells where they were held until they could be put up for sale. They would command a better price if they looked strong and healthy, so slave traders often fed the new arrivals well to improve their appearance. One slave from the early 1800s would later tell how the Africans were readied for an auction:

> *In the first place we were required to wash thoroughly, and those with beards, to shave. We were then furnished with a new suit each, cheap, but clean. . . . We were now conducted into a large room . . . . The men were arranged on one side of the room, the women on the other. . . . Freeman [the trader] . . . exhorted us to appear smart and lively, sometimes threatening, and again, holding out various inducements.*

Every auction day, slaves were sold off to the highest bidders. Plantation owners might identify their newly purchased slaves by branding them. The Africans were then shackled for the journey to whatever distant plantation awaited. Many buyers only sought a single or a few slaves at a time and did not try to buy both a husband and a wife, or a mother with her children. As a result, families were wrenched apart.

RICE IN THE LOWER SOUTH

By the 1700s, the colonies of the Deep South had branched out from tobacco to grow other lucrative cash crops, such as rice and indigo. (Indigo is a dark violet-blue or purple dye.) These plantations needed labor as much as the tobacco plantations had.

These slave girls shuffle rice stalks with their bare feet to separate the rice grains from the rest of the plant.

Slave traders soon realized that offering slaves from the rice-growing regions of Africa could boost sales. Meanwhile, the enslaved Africans brought with them some of their own methods for growing rice, which may have improved the harvests of the Southern rice plantations.

Rice cultivation was hard and dangerous. Slaves had to clear acres of mudflats (coastal wetlands). Next, they dug miles of ditches using picks and shovels. The ditches would become canals both for bringing in tidal water and for draining the fields. The slaves would then build levees (walls of dirt) to surround the fields. The work of growing rice began

When cultivating rice, slaves labored in wetlands, which bred alligators and poisonous snakes that would become trapped by the levees. The water also hatched millions of mosquitoes that could carry deadly yellow fever and malaria.

in April and continued into late autumn. It involved planting, alternately flooding and draining the fields, weeding, harvesting, and threshing (separating rice grains from the harvested plants).

It is estimated that in the 18th century, as many as one-third of slaves newly arrived in the rice fields died within a year. Not only was the work deadly, but the living conditions for the slaves probably weakened them. They lived in wooden shacks that were prone to fires. While some slaveholders provided enough boiled rice, cornmeal, molasses, and butter or bacon fat for the slaves to eat, others did not. If slaves wanted more, they had to tend beans or yams or go fishing at the end of their weary workday. Although many plantations had sick rooms or hospitals for the slaves, the doctors did not know how to treat fevers and diseases.

THE KING OF DYE

The Low Country of coastal South Carolina and Georgia also supported the growing of indigo. In Europe, indigo dye and paint gained great popularity, but indigo could not be grown in Europe's temperate climate. Spain, France, and England therefore turned to their New World colonies.

Growing indigo required skilled laborers. Since indigo grew in parts of Africa, enterprising slave traders could provide

African slaves who had the needed skills. By the mid-1700s, plantations in South Carolina were producing shiploads of the dye. About 60 slaves would work on an indigo plantation.

Rice and indigo were sometimes grown on the same plantation. As Governor James Glen of South Carolina wrote in 1761, "both Indigo and Rice may be managed by the same Persons, for the Labor attending Indigo being over the Summer Months, those who were employed in it may afterwards manufacture Rice in the ensuing Part of the Year, when it becomes most laborious."

AFRICAN FOLKTALES, AFRICAN DRUMS

Despite such brutal workdays, slaves still found moments to build a common culture. Back in the slave quarters, they gathered around their fires, shared their one-pot meals, tended their vegetables, and put their children to bed.

Folktales and music played important roles in African tribal life. Through folktales and songs, storytellers passed along tribal history and beliefs from one generation to the next. In the New World, African slaves changed the stories slightly to fit their new circumstances, but the basic messages were the same. In the stories, the weak (such as enslaved people) could use their wits and good character to win the day against the strong (slaveholders). Some of those folktales have been preserved to the present day in the Br'er (Brother) Rabbit stories. Among the slaves, Br'er Rabbit's trickery in outsmarting Br'er Fox symbolized their own resistance to white owners and overseers.

In a similar way, the slaves reproduced the music of their past. Some African Americans learned to play European instruments, such as the flute and the violin. Many more African Americans created instruments like those of their African tribes. One favorite instrument was the drum. In South Carolina, the white population feared that slaves would use the drum to send secret messages. To prevent this, whites passed a law prohibiting slaves from "using or keeping drums, horns, or other loud instruments. . . ."

Equally popular with slaves and less frightening to the slaveholders were the banjo and a xylophone-type instrument known as a *balafo*. To make the *balafo*, African Americans fastened thin wooden slats of various lengths above numerous, different-sized gourds.

BORN IN AMERICA

A large majority of the slaves imported to the Americas before 1776 went to Brazil and the West Indies. Only about 5 to 6 percent arrived on the shores of the British colonies of North America. Yet by the first years of the American Revolution (1775–1783), 263,000 people of African descent had been forcibly imported to the colonies.

As conflict grew between England and its colonies, African Americans, both slave and free, listened to the language of "freedom from tyranny" with great excitement. Although the American Revolution would not lead immediately to emancipation, it would plant new seeds of hope and courage in the hearts of the enslaved African Americans.

4

Slavery in the New Nation

Slaves were bought and sold at auctions throughout the United States,
even after the American Revolution. Although many Americans had
won their freedom from Great Britain, slaves remained the property of
their masters.

THE DESIRE FOR LIBERTY

By the 1760s, after war with France both in the colonies and in Europe, England had accumulated an enormous war debt. The British lawmaking body, Parliament, claimed that the war in America had been in defense of the colonies, so the colonists should help pay the expenses. Parliament proceeded to pass one law after another, creating new taxes for the colonists.

This picture of the Boston Massacre helped fuel the fires of revolution. It shows the British firing on civilians while several lie dying on the ground.

The American colonists raised loud protests. In response, the British sent 4,000 troops to the colonies. The presence of British troops on American soil angered many colonists. By 1770, colonial protests led to violence.

On the evening of March 5, 1770, British troops in Boston, Massachusetts, faced a group that a newspaper editor would later call "a motley rabble of saucy boys, negroes and mulattoes, Irish teagues [Irishmen] and outlandish tarrs [foreign sailors]." People later reported that the Bostonians had pelted the British soldiers with insults, rocks, sticks, and snowballs. The soldiers allegedly panicked and fired into the crowd, leaving five people dead.

Among the dead was a former slave named Crispus Attucks. Witnesses claimed that Attucks had been the ringleader of the mob and that he was the first to be shot dead. To some, Attucks became a hero, "the first to defy, the first to die." In the hands of the colonial leaders, who felt betrayed by the British government, he became a symbol of liberty. They called the event the Boston Massacre and buried Attucks and the other victims with honor.

James Somerset (1742–unknown)

James Somerset was born in 1742 in West Africa. When he was just eight years old, he was enslaved and taken to Virginia. There, a planter named Charles Steuart bought Somerset and eventually made him a personal servant.

In 1771, Steuart took Somerset with him on a trip to England. While there, Somerset ran away. When he was recaptured, Steuart decided to turn him over to a sea captain bound for Jamaica.

A British abolitionist whose name is unknown managed to free Somerset before the ship could sail. The same abolitionist presented a petition on Somerset's behalf before the British court. A London newspaper reported, "Yesterday the Court of King's Bench gave judgment in the case of Somerset the Negro, finding that Mr. Steuart, his master, had no power to compel him on board a ship, or to send him back to the plantations."

Somerset was set free. For people who saw slaves as personal property, the verdict was shocking. Some misunderstood the judge to say that slavery was ended in England. Slaves from Virginia's plantations were soon on the run, seeking passage on any ship bound for the English capital of London.

A POET FOR FREEDOM

While colonial leaders debated what to do about the oppressive British tax laws, African Americans became bolder on behalf of their own freedom from oppression. In 1772, a surprising voice emerged in Boston. A young slave named Phillis Wheatley, kidnapped in Africa and taken to Boston in 1761, published a poem in support of the colonies' quest for liberty. She addressed her poem to the Earl of Dartmouth, William Legge, who had just been appointed by the British king to deal with the rebellious colonies. Wheatley explained the source of her love of freedom:

> I, young in life, by seeming cruel fate
> Was snatch'd from Afric's fancy'd happy seat:
> What pangs excruciating must molest,
> What sorrows labour in my parent's breast? . . .
> Such, such my case. And can I then but pray
> Others may never feel tyrannic sway?

One year later, Wheatley published a book of poems called *Poems on Various Subjects.* Only two women had published a book of poems in America before Wheatley, and neither was African American or a slave. Thanks to her frail health and the kindness of her owners, she spent her youth studying languages, literature, and theology. When she published her book, her owners emancipated her.

Wheatley was not the only African American speaking out. In 1773, a committee of slaves in Massachusetts sent a petition to the colonial government, requesting freedom so they could emigrate to Africa. "We cannot but wish and hope," they wrote, "that you will have the same grand object, we mean civil and religious liberty, in view in your next [legislative] session." Petitions from other African-American groups followed, and all were denied.

Southern slaves, meanwhile, were usually forbidden to learn writing and reading. Although some found ways of learning anyway, most relied on the spoken word. One preacher, born in Africa and remembered only as "David," met with a group of black and white Christians in Charleston, South Carolina, in 1775. God would deliver the slaves from the power of their masters in the coming conflict, he promised, just as God had freed the children of Israel from bondage in Egypt. Messages like this would be repeated by many others over the war years.

THE REVOLUTION AND ITS AFTERMATH

The American Revolution lasted from 1775 to 1783. The colonists who wanted complete independence were known as Patriots. Those who remained loyal to the British king were called Loyalists. African Americans fought on both the Patriot and the Loyalist sides of the conflict because both sides promised emancipation in return.

The first battles of the war occurred in Lexington and Concord in 1775, and African Americans were among the Patriot forces there. Later that year, George Washington took command of the Continental army. Washington, who himself owned more than 200 slaves, prohibited recruitment of black soldiers. He worried that colonists in the Deep South would lose their enthusiasm for the Patriot cause if African Americans were recruited.

In the winter of 1777–1778, Washington changed his mind. By then, his army was dwindling as men deserted, fell ill, or were killed in battle. So Washington officially approved the recruitment of black soldiers. Before the war ended, approximately 5,000 black men would serve in the colonial army, with hundreds of others in the colonial navy.

One of many black soldiers to serve in the American Revolution assists the Marquis de Lafayette as he directs a battle against the British.

As it turned out, more blacks eventually served on the side of England than on the colonial side. The British promised freedom and the chance to leave America. Thousands of slaves ran away from Southern plantations, hoping to reach British ships that would carry them to Canada or England.

However, British promises were not all they appeared to be. When blacks who joined the British fell ill or were injured, the British removed them from the army camps, leaving them to heal or die on their own. In the final battles of the war in Virginia, the British pushed their black soldiers to the front lines, ahead of the whites, where many of the former slaves were soon killed.

After the British surrendered, Americans gathered the surviving blacks to return the slaves among them to their masters. As the British ships retreated from Southern ports, runaway slaves flocked to board them. There were stories that when African Americans attempted to clamber aboard, British sailors hacked at them with cutlasses rather than let them on the ships.

On the other hand, British commander Sir Guy Carleton refused to meet George Washington's demand that American property, including slaves, be returned to the Americans. As the British evacuated the colonies, Carleton extended his protection to Loyalist slaves. An estimated 3,000 to 4,000 successfully boarded ships in New York City, bound for Jamaica, Nova Scotia, and Britain.

Americans now needed to create a government. Each state wrote a constitution of its own, and the Continental Congress, a group of representatives from all the former colonies, created a constitution for the United States.

The ideals of "life, liberty, and pursuit of happiness" that had driven the colonial bid for independence made many white Americans rethink slavery, especially in the North, where wealth was not so dependent on slave labor. In 1777, Vermont became the first state in the Union to abolish slavery outright. In 1780, Pennsylvania enacted a law that said the children of enslaved mothers would become free at a certain age. In that same year, Massachusetts passed a state constitution stating that everyone is "born free and equal." In 1783, a Massachusetts judge interpreted this statement in favor of a slave's right to be free, essentially ending slavery in that state.

Connecticut and Rhode Island followed with gradual emancipation in 1784, and New York in 1804.

NEW IDENTITIES, CHANGING TIMES

The spread of emancipation in the North gradually turned slavery into a Southern institution. In the Chesapeake region, where there were large slave populations, the idealism of the American Revolution and religious objections to slavery led to a sizable free black community. However, racism grew. Free black Americans could rarely get good jobs, move freely into white neighborhoods, serve on juries, or vote.

To help themselves with these problems, free African Americans created neighborhoods, churches, clubs, and schools of their own. They got what education they could, learning trades and forming mutual-aid societies to support one another.

Meanwhile, three events occurred that would keep slavery going in the South. First, in 1793, came the invention of the cotton gin, which made it possible for cotton workers to prepare 50 times as much raw cotton in a day as they could by hand. Cotton, which was highly desired in Europe, quickly became the king of commercial crops in the South.

Second, because of the explosive growth of cotton as a cash crop, slave traders found that the market for slaves from Africa was stronger than ever. Between 1793 and 1807, more than 100,000 slaves were imported to the cotton-growing region of the United States from Africa.

Third, the young United States unexpectedly had the opportunity to double its territory. To the west of the new nation lay the Louisiana Territory, an area under French control. The territory stretched from the Mississippi River west to the Rocky Mountains and north to Canada. U.S. leaders wanted to expand settlement into that territory. They knew they would need to control the port of New Orleans and the Mississippi River in order to do so. When the United States asked to buy New Orleans from the French, France's ruler, Napoleon Bonaparte, offered to sell the entire Louisiana Territory. On December 20, 1803, the Louisiana Purchase allowed the United States to raise its flag over New Orleans.

> U.S. census records indicate that in the two decades from 1790 to 1810, the black population of the South nearly doubled, from 690,061 to 1,268,499. In 1808, Congress banned the importation of slaves, but smugglers continued to sneak Africans into the country.

This painting depicts James Monroe and French officials signing the Louisiana Purchase with a map of the southern colonies and territories of the United States painted above.

For three cents per acre (0.4 ha), the United States had opened the sprawling heartland of the North American continent to exploration, settlement, and development. Suddenly, the land was open to slavery as well.

5

The Growth of Plantations in the Deep South

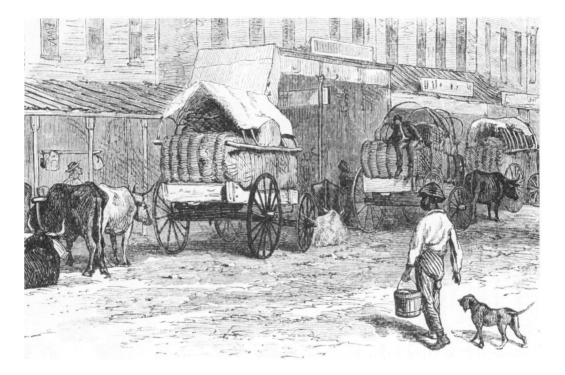

In this illustration of a rural town, a wagon train leaves filled with cotton from Southern plantations. As the demand for cotton increased to feed the textile mills of the North, Southern cotton growers required more and more slaves to work their plantations.

THE COTTON BOOM

Before the cotton gin's arrival, slaveholders who had been raising tobacco, rice, and indigo began to see the market for their products decline. Without a strong market, it became too expensive to keep their slaves. Some slaveholders began to free their slaves just to save money.

With the creation of the cotton gin, cotton production multiplied. Other inventions also helped the textile industry grow. In New England, textile mills suddenly had machines that could spin and weave the cotton at great speed. Steam power allowed boats to transport both the raw cotton and the finished cotton cloth cheaply. By the mid-1800s, cotton would be the single most important cash crop in the United States.

With the great expansion of cotton production, planters no longer wanted to get rid of their slaves. Many planters moved to the cotton regions of Georgia and South Carolina's Sea Islands or the subtropics of Louisiana and Mississippi. In the Upper South, slave populations continued to grow, and some slaveholders there sold their slaves south at great profit. To a greater extent than ever before, slave-dependent plantations became big business, creating wealth for their owners. As a result, whites continued to exploit the labor of African-American slaves on a grand scale.

The cotton gin consisted of a boxed cylinder on which were mounted spiked teeth. A crank was used to turn the cylinder, and the teeth separated the seeds from the cotton fiber. Before the cotton gin, slaves picked each seed out of the cotton by hand.

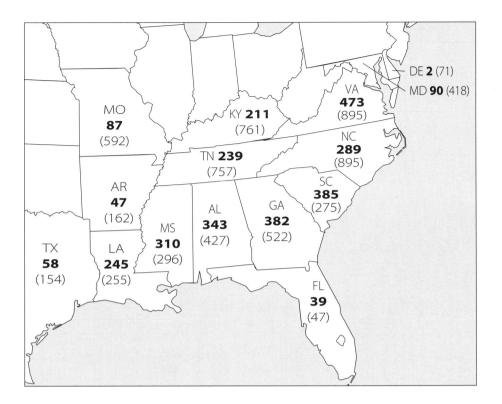

This map shows the slave population of the southern and border states according to the 1850 U.S. Census. Numbers are in thousands. Each state's white population is indicated in parenthesis.

THE COTTON PLANTATION

Like rice and sugar, cotton was a labor-intensive business that kept enslaved African Americans working the fields year-round. In March and April, slaves prepared the soil and planted the cotton. Tending the plants and hoeing kept the slaves busy from April through August. They had to thin the cotton plants and pull the weeds and grass from the rows. In late August, picking began, continuing until the end of January.

In January and February, the slaves would gin and press the cotton, then load it into wagons and drive it to the docks for shipping. Come March, the whole process started over again.

The huge cotton plantations of Louisiana and Mississippi depended primarily on gang labor. With hundreds of slaves to coordinate, planters organized the workers into gangs, or groups, according to the type of work they were doing. There were hoe gangs, plow gangs, and gangs who picked the cotton, all spurred along by the driver, whose job it was to keep everyone moving as quickly as possible.

Cotton Quotas

The owners determined the amount of cotton that a slave should be able to pick in a day. At the end of a day, slaves carried their sacks or baskets back to a large scale. As Solomon Northup, a Sea Island slave, later explained,

> If it falls short in weight . . . [the slave] knows that he must suffer. And if he has exceeded it by ten or twenty pounds [4.5 or 9 kg], in all probability his master will measure the next day's task accordingly. So whether he has too little or too much, his approach to the gin-house is always with fear and trembling. . . . After weighing, follow the whippings.

Slaves were also responsible for spinning thread out of the cotton. These slaves were usually women who had recently had babies and were not yet able to go back to the fields. They, too, had to produce a set amount. If they were short, they were whipped.

The driver answered to the overseer, who made sure that production remained at the highest possible level. If any slaves (man, woman, or child) slowed the work in any way, the overseer applied physical punishment that would make them reluctant to ever do so again. He might use a whip or a cobbing board, which was a paddle with holes drilled into it to raise blisters when a person was beaten. If he caught slaves trying to run away, he would first punish them, then make them wear iron collars, iron head gear, or chains.

In addition to the work of growing cotton, slaves had to clear new land, dig ditches, and cut and haul wood. They worked on the plantation as mechanics, butchers, blacksmiths, carpenters, and drivers. Slave women cared for their masters' children, spun, wove, and sewed their masters' clothing, and cooked for their masters' family. Some slaves worked in the masters' houses as domestic or personal servants.

Most important for the community life of the slaves were the slave quarters, the cabins that housed slave families. It was there, out of sight and sound of the big house, that slaves kept a separate culture alive.

LIFE ON THE SEA ISLANDS

The African Americans of the Sea Islands had lives that were isolated from the rest of the world. A large number of people who were just arrived from Africa were slaves there. In the three years after importation became illegal in 1808, South Carolina imported at least an additional 23,773 slaves. As a result, the slave culture of the Sea Islands was strong.

African Americans had their own class system that developed out of the different roles they played on the large plantations. The slaves most respected (and feared) within the slave community were the drivers. These black men worked under white overseers to manage the plantation. They directed and punished field hands and handed out rations of food and supplies.

Next in line were the tradesmen. These skilled workers labored as carpenters, blacksmiths, coopers, wheelwrights, and so on. On occasion, owners would hire out their enslaved tradesmen to neighboring planters, giving these African Americans more freedom of movement and exposure to other influences.

A Language of Their Own

Sea Island slaves spoke a unique Creole language known as Gullah, probably named for Angola, from which many of them came. Gullah combined English words with pronunciations and sentence structures from African languages. The language gave the black people a way of communicating with each other that was hard for the white people of the plantation to understand.

Many of the Gullah words were actually a string of words. For example, the word for "mechanic" sounded like "beet on ayun," which literally meant "beat on iron." An honest person was called a "troot ma-wt," which was literally "truth mouth." A preacher was a "tebl tappa," or "table tapper." A cemetery was a "sho ded," or "sure dead."

Some Gullah words have found their way into everyday English. *Goober* (another word for peanut), *gumbo* (a kind of stew), and *yam* all come from Gullah.

The house servants came next in importance. Like the tradesmen, they had a direct role in the lives of the white people. Because they were in constant contact with the planter's family, they heard a lot about what was happening in the rest of the world. They carried news, as well as the hand-me-down clothes given to them by the master's family, back to the slave quarters. The other slaves sometimes distrusted the house slaves, fearful that they might report slave activities to the slaveholders in the big house.

At the lowest end of the slave hierarchy were the field hands. Sea Island cotton workers labored under a "task system." This meant that the overseer assigned them a specific amount of work to accomplish in a day. When that work was completed, they could leave the field and take care of their own chores. Usually, field hands were given about a quarter of an acre (0.1 ha) on which they could grow food—corn, potatoes, yams, or beans—to add to their rations. They also were permitted to raise chickens, pigs, and ducks.

AFRICAN-AMERICAN MEDICINE

Although the planters provided medical care for the slaves, African Americans often preferred the herbal cures they had brought with them from Africa. At that time, the favorite white cure for just about any ailment was bloodletting—the practice of letting the ailing person bleed. Doctors believed that bleeding helped restore a body's balance and good health. The slave community preferred to rely on its "doctor women" or "grannies" instead. These healers created broths using leaves, bark, twigs, turpentine, tobacco, or catnip to cure virtually anything, from toothaches to whooping cough.

The slaves also looked to conjurers (also known as "witch doctors" or "root doctors") for guidance. The slaves believed that conjurers could read omens and dreams, cast spells, and make good luck charms or hexes. The people feared their conjurers as much as they respected them. Nevertheless, turning to their own instead of depending on what the slaveholders offered helped to hold the slave community together.

THE SLAVE FAMILY

Southern slaves' plantation quarters often allowed them to live as individual families, unlike the slaves on Caribbean plantations, who lived in barracks-style group houses. Many Southern slaveholders encouraged their slaves to make families. After all, when the slaves had babies, the slaveholder obtained additional slaves without having to purchase them.

Slaveholders knew as well that family ties made slaves less inclined to escape. The blacks knew that if they ran away, they might never see their families again. Furthermore, their families might be punished in their place. If a fugitive slave was caught, the slaveholder could easily decide to sell him or her away from the plantation in order to be rid of a troublemaker.

Even without such cause, slaveholders often chose to sell slaves away for other reasons. This reality inflicted terrible suffering on enslaved people. They never knew whether they would wake up one morning to find that a family member was gone for good. In some cases, children were sold right out of their mothers' arms.

Slave families were further distressed by the extremely exhausting and sometimes dangerous types of work they were required to do. The life span of a slave was generally not long, especially for those who worked on large plantations. However, early death could occur anywhere, because most slaves were subjected to poor nutrition, illness, overwork, and severe punishments.

One slave prays for himself and his family as a slave trader leads another slave away to a sailing ship.

As a result, the slave community learned to create family connections that could replace those that were stolen from them. When a parent died, for example, an aunt, uncle, or friend would take on the job of parenting the child left behind. Within the community of enslaved African Americans, people routinely called older women "mother" or "auntie," older men "father" or "uncle," and people of similar age "sister" and "brother." They took pains to know as much as they could of their family members so they could continue to maintain their connections. Their strong belief in the spiritual power of their ancestors in everyday life made these connections all the more important to them.

IN LIFE AND DEATH

African Americans continued many of the traditions of Africa in the way they lived, and they did the same at the time of someone's death. The burial rituals of the blacks reflected their beliefs about what happens to people after they die. The rituals also gave the living within the slave community a strong sense of their common heritage.

For instance, because the slaves (and their African ancestors) believed that the world is oriented from east to west, following the sun, they would lay deceased people in coffins with their faces turned toward the east. To make sure that the dead people's spirits were released from the body, the African Americans would take dishes and earthenware vessels that the deceased had used and break them on the grave. This, they believed, would "break the chains of death."

Slaves decorated their gravesites with shells or mirrors. Both objects symbolized water and represented the African belief that the realm of the dead exists beneath river bottoms.

The blacks also placed white objects, such as pieces of white china or figures carved from white stone, on the graves. This practice reflected their belief that a dead family member would become a white creature called a *bakulu* who could return to the living unseen and direct their lives.

A group of slaves gathers for a funeral and burial. One of the group, probably a preacher, speaks to the mourners while others kneel and weep near the coffin.

THE MIGRATION OF SLAVES

When the United States finally banned the international slave trade in 1808, it set in motion a new period of cruelty to slave families. The ban occurred just at the time that cotton and sugar plantations were expanding at a great rate across the Louisiana Territory. At the same time, the declining market for tobacco made slavery less important to the states of the Upper South.

Slaveholders of the Upper South saw that they could make money from slaves they no longer needed by selling them down the Ohio and Mississippi Rivers. Plantations were being built all along the banks of the rivers and across the countryside, and they needed more slaves.

Being sold was one more occasion when African Americans felt the terrible cruelty of being considered property instead of human beings. They would be sold south by the hundreds of thousands, and most often, they would not go as families. Those precious family connections they had worked so hard to forge would have to be reinvented.

6

Slavery in the Antebellum Upper South

For some, the grand mansions of rich slave owners represent the best
of the pre–Civil War South. For others, they stand in stark contrast to
the conditions under which most slaves lived.

BEFORE THE WAR

In the decades from 1820 to 1860, known as the antebellum (literally, "before the war") period, life for African Americans became more varied. In the Northern states, slavery had been abolished or changed to a program of gradual emancipation. New opportunities for education, employment, and property ownership opened up in limited ways for blacks.

Unfortunately, racial prejudice continued. The Northern states still did not give equal economic and legal rights to free blacks. Most were not allowed to vote, sit on a jury, or receive equal wages for equal work compared to whites.

In the Deep South, millions of blacks endured brutal treatment under white overseers and black slave drivers who were determined to get as much labor—and, therefore, profit—out of the slaves as they could. At the same time, the African Americans faced the constant loss of loved ones and increasingly rigid slave laws designed to keep them under strict control.

In the Upper South, the institution of slavery continued. Yet the profitability of tobacco had declined, so slaves often failed to earn back their costs. For a short time in the early 1800s, numerous slaveholders freed their slaves. As a result, the number of freed African Americans increased substantially in Maryland, Delaware, parts of Virginia, and Washington, D.C.

Some of the freed people chose to travel north, either to states that had abolished slavery or all the way to Canada, where slavery had also been outlawed. Others remained in the Upper South, leasing land from white planters to farm or living near urban areas where plenty of work could be found.

Often, the freed African Americans worked alongside slaves, doing exactly the same work. However, at the end of the day, the free blacks went back to a small house or farm of their own with wages in hand. The slaves returned to the slave quarters.

SLAVES FOR HIRE

Some plantations of the Upper South continued to flourish using slaves. Corn, tobacco, wheat, and livestock often grew on the same plantation, making it possible for planters to turn a profit. In addition, nearly every industry used slave labor for at least some of its work. The early 1800s saw the rise of numerous industries across the South. Stone was quarried, and iron, coal, salt, lead, and gold were mined. Pine forests provided natural resources for timber operations. Brick factories and iron foundries produced building materials for construction and shipbuilding. Virginia had more factories, and more slaves working in the factories, than any other Southern state.

The life of enslaved people in urban areas and in trade work brought them into close contact with the world of white people. They were much more likely than plantation workers to find ways to learn to read and write, to hear the messages of Northern abolitionists, and to see some of the changes taking place among African Americans farther north.

Many slaves acquired trade skills. They became mining engineers, blacksmiths, shoemakers, tailors, boatmen, cabinetmakers, and masons. Some slaveholders then traded on their slaves' skills. In a practice known as "hiring out," the slaveholders sold the slaves' labor but kept the slaves.

For example, when Washington, D.C., became the nation's capital, most of the workforce for the preliminary buildings was hired-out slave labor. The slaveholders received 75 cents a day for each slave. The slaveholders had to give each slave one suit of clothes and a blanket. The U.S. government guaranteed one full meal per slave a day.

Skilled slaves such as wheelwrights, mechanics, carpenters, or seamstresses often had a better chance at finding jobs in Northern cities than escaped field hands.

RUMORS, REVOLTS, AND RUNAWAYS

In 1822, news went out from South Carolina about a slave revolt that had been planned by a former slave named Denmark Vesey. The plot was exposed before it could be carried out, and 35 conspirators, including Vesey, were executed.

From the time of Vesey's attempted revolt, Southern communities began to enforce their slave laws more strictly and put new, harsher laws in place. However, in Virginia in 1831, a religious slave named Nat Turner fulfilled his own dream that God had called him to lead African-American slaves against their white owners. Before Turner was stopped, he and a growing crowd of slaves killed about 60 white men, women, and children, leaving terror in their wake.

As much as whites feared the anger of the people they had enslaved, they had little violent rebellion to deal with. Overall, North American slaves remained a minority, without the power to free themselves by force. In reality, most slaves rebelled quietly. They pretended not to understand orders, worked as slowly as they dared, claimed to be ill, or ran away, even if it were only for a few days.

An increasing number of slaves made a run for permanent freedom in the years leading up to the Civil War (1861–1865). People who opposed slavery in the North and South developed a network that offered fugitive slaves shelter, food, and clothing along a number of northbound routes. The network came to be known as the Underground Railroad. The ultimate goal for most slaves was Canada, where they felt relatively safe from people who would want to send them back to their former masters.

Nat Turner and other slaves are shown planning their rebellion in this illustration from 1863.

Southern states such as Kentucky and Delaware organized extensive slave patrols in hope of stopping the northern flow of fugitives. Such was the determination and desperation of the African Americans that although many were caught and sent back, no one ever succeeded in closing the routes to freedom.

SLAVE CODES

Every slave state of the South had slave laws, or Black Codes, that dictated what African Americans, both enslaved and free, could and could not do. In some cases, the laws protected the enslaved. The laws required that slaveholders feed, clothe, and shelter their slaves. They could not legally maim or kill a slave, except in self-defense. On the other hand, the death penalty had been used since the 17th century against slaves who plotted rebellion or hurt white people. The codes were also intended to protect the institution of slavery, keeping whites firmly in control and the slaves hard at work.

Sophia Bell (unknown–unknown)

Sophia Bell was a hired-out slave in Washington, D.C. Although she was a slave, Sophia grew a small garden of her own and sold the produce. Over time, she secretly saved $400, the price to buy the freedom of her husband, George. After working a few years as a freedman, George was then able to save enough to buy Sophia's freedom.

The Bells went on saving, and over a number of years, they purchased the freedom of numerous other family members who proceeded to do the same. The Bell family liberated through purchase about 24 members of their clan. In 1807, with two other free blacks, George and Sophia opened the first school for African Americans in Washington, D.C.

All slave codes included restrictions on how late a slave could be out at night. These laws posed a particular problem for husbands and wives who lived in different locations, as many did. Married slaves sometimes lived quite a distance from each other. The only time they could visit was from Saturday afternoon to Sunday evening, making it almost impossible to return in time to obey the code.

Slave Patrols

African Americans called the men who patrolled throughout the South, enforcing the slave codes, "patterollers." These men would stop any African American, slave or free, anywhere and demand to see a pass. They also had the responsibility to hunt down escaped slaves and return them to their home plantations. To do this, the patterollers worked in groups of at least five men and often used dogs. The immediate punishment, enacted on the spot by a patteroller, was a whipping.

One former slave named Jane Pyatt later remembered,

Previous to 1861, there weren't any policemen . . . [there] were patterollers instead. . . . If the slaves had a corn shucking party . . . and if they made too much noise, the patterollers would arrest them. . . . These patterollers took two of my brothers. . . . I have never seen them since.

It is possible that Pyatt's brothers had evaded slave laws once too often and were sold South as a result.

All free blacks had to carry papers with them at all times proving that they were free. Furthermore, any slave moving around the countryside had to have written permission to do so in the form of a pass. In either case, it was assumed that blacks were runaway slaves unless they could prove otherwise. If a slaveholder did not claim the supposed runaways within a certain period of time, they would be sold at auction, even if they were actually free.

Many states' Black Codes made it illegal to teach slaves to read and write, although this law was not always enforced. Others banned slaves from gathering in groups. In some states, blacks could not attend a church unless the minister was white or a certain number of white people were in attendance. Blacks could not trade, buy, or sell without written permission. They could not carry arms.

In South Carolina, one of the states with a relatively large slave population, the death penalty was established for a variety of offenses: plotting insurrections, committing arson, making or using poisons, murder, and running away. The state also prohibited slaves from owning livestock or hiring themselves out and banned new arrivals of free African Americans.

Although some slave codes appeared to protect slaves from excessive punishment and other injustices, the laws were most likely to be enforced in favor of whites. As abolition gained popularity in the North and Southerners grew more tense about their own safety, the slave laws became increasingly harsh and were more strictly observed.

FRONTIER FARMS

When slaveholding Americans moved westward from the Upper South, they took their slaves with them. The farms and plantations in regions such as Kentucky tended to be smaller than those in the Deep South, so few farmers held more than 10 slaves. The slaves usually built their own quarters, which were rustic cabins containing only a table, a chair, and a built-in bed frame that they filled with straw or corn husks. They made family out of the other slaves.

The best times in the slave community happened around events such as corn shuckings, hog killings, or weddings, which Kentucky slaveholders permitted. These occasions became an excuse for parties, dances, and religious services, giving slaves who lived far apart a chance to gather and socialize.

Slaves in Kentucky were well known for the music they made. Playing music helped them to find relief from their toil on the plantations. Whites enjoyed the music and often expected the slaves to perform for their guests in the big house.

Probably the best known of the antebellum African-American musical performers was a slave named Jim Crow. He worked in a livery stable that hired out horses and carriages in Louisville, Kentucky. To amuse customers while they waited, he would sing and dance for them.

Crow became so popular that a white actor decided to copy his act. He borrowed old clothes, blackened his face, and performed Crow's music onstage. This style of performance, in "blackface," remained popular for another 100 years. After the Civil War, when the former slave states created laws that discriminated against African Americans, people attached Jim Crow's famous name to the laws.

THE SOUTHERN CHURCHES OF AFRICAN AMERICANS

In the Upper South of the 1800s, some important changes began to take place. The Methodist denomination did much to bring African Americans more fully into traditional Christian practices. Methodist ministers often traveled throughout the countryside to make new converts to Christianity. Some slave owners welcomed Christian conversion for their slaves because they believed it might encourage blacks to be more obedient to their owners.

These slaves were photographed on their way to church on Folly Island, South Carolina, in 1860.

Over time, an increasing number of black leaders gained opportunities to preach to black congregations. Black Methodist and Baptist congregations became more common, and a number of formal associations of black churches developed.

Southern white ministers taught that the Bible commanded slaves to be obedient to their masters. Instead of obedience to masters, black preachers spoke of eventual freedom, comparing the slave community to the Old Testament Israelites in slavery in Egypt. Just as God had delivered his people to the Promised Land of old, so would God deliver the African-American slaves from bondage. Religious meetings and gatherings also offered new opportunities for slaves to gain some formal education.

Meanwhile, some African Americans continued combining Christian beliefs with elements of African religions. To this purpose, slaves throughout the South often sneaked away from their quarters after dark to meet in the woods and conduct their own meetings. There, they performed the songs and dances, shouts and prayers that would not have been accepted in white churches and gatherings.

THE SLAVE TRADE CONTINUES

As the demand for slaves leveled off and declined in the Upper South, it expanded dramatically in the Deep South. Many slaveholders in the Upper South began to realize that they could make a greater profit by selling their slaves to Deep South plantations than by using them as forced labor.

The most unscrupulous of slaveholders actually encouraged their enslaved people to have babies so that the youngsters could be sold away. Other slaveholders may have been less ruthless, but their willingness to sell their slaves south for profit had the same tragic consequences for the African Americans.

7

Preparing for Freedom

One of the most powerful forces against slavery was the written word. Harriet Beecher Stowe's book, *Uncle Tom's Cabin*, popularized the idea of freedom for the slaves. This illustration from the book shows former slaves celebrating their freedom.

FIGHTING OVER SLAVERY

By the 1830s and 1840s, slaveholders in great numbers had moved west into Arkansas, Louisiana, Mississippi, and Texas. American Indians who had formerly lived there had been driven farther west, freeing ample space for vast cotton and sugar holdings. Alabama, Mississippi, and Louisiana became the heart of the cotton kingdom, producing half the nation's supply of cotton by mid-century.

During the same period, the Northern states were slowly but surely bringing slavery to an end. A great division developed over the question of whether slavery would be allowed to continue and spread. To address the question, Congress passed legislation in 1850 that accepted a limit on the spread of slavery in the West while protecting the rights and "property" (slaves) of existing slaveholders in the South.

Meanwhile, in 1852, an abolitionist named Harriet Beecher Stowe published a novel called *Uncle Tom's Cabin.* The book, which tells the story of a slave family and its struggles for freedom, became an instant best seller in the North. For many Northerners, it was the first exposure to the worst cruelties of slavery. Southerners claimed that Stowe's picture of slavery was much worse than reality. The book, which was banned in many areas of the South, hardened opinions about slavery on both sides.

The country soon faced violence over the future of slavery. The territory of Kansas turned into a bloody battleground between proslavery and antislavery forces in 1855. Then, in 1859, at Harpers Ferry, Virginia, an abolitionist named John Brown staged an attack on a federal armory, intending to take it by force so he could arm slaves for violent insurrection. Brown's raid failed, but not before numerous people had died, and Brown was taken captive by the U.S. Marines. His execution some months later made him a popular martyr for the cause of abolition.

Newspapers throughout the country carried accounts of John Brown's raid and execution, such as this illustration from *John Leslie's Illustrated Newspaper,* November 5, 1859.

SLAVERY SPLITS THE NATION

In 1860, Abraham Lincoln won the presidential election with less than 40 percent of the popular vote. By then, the nation was hopelessly divided, and although the arguments focused

In 1860, one-half of all Southerners were either slaves or members of slaveholding families. About 11,000 families held more than 50 slaves. More than 3,000 families held more than 100 slaves.

on states' rights, the heart of the problem was slavery.

The South had become a society that depended on slavery for its economic well-being. Southerners would not voluntarily end or limit slavery. The Democratic Party, especially in the South, believed that individual states possessed the right to decide for themselves whether to be slave states or free states. However, the Republican Party in the North claimed that the nation must stand united to halt the spread of slavery or fall divided.

Before the election year was over, South Carolina decided that the United States, divided as it was over slavery, must fall. Delegates at a state convention unanimously voted that South Carolina should secede from the United States. Mississippi, Florida, Alabama, Georgia, Louisiana, and Texas promptly followed South Carolina's lead. Together, the seven seceded states established the Confederate States of America, or Confederacy, and elected Jefferson Davis of Mississippi as president.

In April 1861, Confederate troops fired on Fort Sumter in South Carolina, forcing the surrender of Union troops. The only casualty at Fort Sumter was a horse, but the conflict marked the beginning of the Civil War. In the aftermath, four more Southern states seceded. With the secession of Virginia, Arkansas, North Carolina, and Tennessee, the Confederacy was complete.

WAR COMES TO THE SOUTH

The Civil War would eventually lead to the abolition of slavery, the single greatest good to come out of America's bloodiest war. Yet not all of the soon-to-be-freed slaves understood what was going on during the war years. Tens of thousands of slaves lived on inland plantations of the Deep South, isolated from the rest of the world. Others heard from their owners that Union soldiers would capture them and sell them away. It took some time for the word to spread that freedom lay within reach.

The slaveholders, on the other hand, understood only too well that their way of life was threatened. Some of them joined the fight as soldiers. Some worked to supply the Confederate army with food, clothes, and munitions. Others focused on protecting their property from the Union army.

The Union waged war from both sea and land, hoping to cut off supplies to the South from the Atlantic Ocean and the Mississippi River. The U.S. Navy established a blockade along the southeastern coast to prevent armaments from being shipped from England. At the same time, the Union army moved to take possession of key Southern cities and cut overland supply lines.

As Southern men went off to fight, many of them left behind not only their wives and children but also their slaves. Other plantation owners deserted their estates as the Union approached, taking as many of their slaves with them as they could. One former slave who was a child during the war later recalled, "I [remember] when they said the Yankees [Northerners] was [coming] the boss man put us in wagons and runned us to Texas. They put the women and [children] in the wagons but the men had to walk."

The slaveholders hoped to keep the slaves from running for freedom behind Union lines. They also wanted to protect their human property from being enlisted by the Confederate army. The Confederates would not arm the African Americans, but used them extensively for the heavy labor of clearing ground, building fortifications, and serving the needs of the white troops. Coastal planters with large holdings of slaves sought refuge in Alabama, the mountains of Tennessee, Georgia, North Carolina, the Deep South, and even the far reaches of Texas.

This illustration shows Confederate soldiers forcing slaves to load cannons for the attack on Fort Sumter that began the Civil War in 1861.

Many African-American men, both free and enslaved, wanted to join the Union forces as full-fledged soldiers and sailors. At first, the Union permitted blacks to be involved only behind the scenes, doing the work of servants and laborers. Not until Abraham Lincoln signed the Emancipation Proclamation on January 1, 1863, officially freeing all enslaved people who were held in Confederate territory, did African Americans gain the right to carry guns and fight.

The black soldiers in the Civil War became the U.S. Colored Troops. By the end of the war, historians believe that as many as 190,000 African Americans (many of them former slaves) served as soldiers and sailors. About 38,000 died from wounds or disease. The black troops fought bravely and earned respect. When the war ended in 1865, one observer named Isaac Johnson described U.S. Colored Troops of liberation coming into North Carolina. "Colored soldiers in Yankee uniforms marched by," he said. "They stepped like lords and conquerors."

The African Americans of the South responded to the war in a variety of ways. Some free blacks chose to support the Confederacy, hoping to safeguard their homes and property. Some slaves remained with the families who held them, frightened by stories of Union soldiers raiding plantations. Some slaves and the families who enslaved them worked together to hide their precious supplies of food and valuables before the Union troops passed through. "The Yankees took about everything," a former slave would remember of the Union troops. "[It was] very difficult to survive."

When Union leaders finally decided they should actively help slaves escape, they hoped to prevent that kind of home-front resistance. Even before the Union made the decision, thousands of enslaved African Americans became refugees seeking freedom behind Union lines or escaping to the North. The numbers only grew larger as the war continued. Everywhere the Union forces went, they were met by slaves hoping to be freed.

THE CURRENCY OF WAR

While the war dragged on, the cotton plantations of the Deep South, which were far removed from the military action, continued their production. Cotton was the South's currency. The Confederate leaders traded it with England for badly needed guns and supplies for the war effort. For the slaves of the cotton plantations, life continued as always.

As the Civil War progressed, the Northern blockade became more effective, and the South could no longer depend on supplies from England. At that point, the Confederate government urged planters to replace some of their cotton with food crops. As a slogan in a Southern newspaper expressed it, "Plant Corn and Be Free, or plant cotton and be whipped." For the slaves who did not run away, nothing changed.

As rumors of the Union army's movements circulated and slaves learned of others who had found freedom behind Union lines, the idea of escape became more believable. Enslaved African Americans did not dare discuss such ideas openly for fear of punishment. Instead, they turned to other means of communication, such as incorporating specific messages of escape routes and freedom into their songs.

SONGS OF SLAVERY

Music held a central place in the day-to-day lives of African-American plantation workers. They sang to make their endless days of labor less grim. As the gangs worked, they used their music to keep a rhythmic motion going. At the end of the day, they sang traditional songs to remember the ways and wisdom of their ancestors. In their celebrations, they joined together in gospel music that called on the Christian God who promised deliverance to the enslaved.

A group of slaves gathers to sing and dance on a Southern plantation in the 1850s.

Hundreds of thousands of slaves were sold south to Mississippi and Louisiana during the Civil War, in part to keep them far from the Union forces who would free them. Though some slaves were transported by ships or railroads, slave traders ordinarily marched the slaves in groups of about 50, called coffles. In a coffle, the slaves were chained together and forced to walk hundreds of miles, sometimes taking a month or more to reach their destination. Almost all of these enslaved people left family and friends behind. Such separations were so common an experience that "The Coffle Song" became a favorite on the Deep South plantations:

Oh! Fare ye well, my bonny love,
I'm gwine away to leave you.
A long farewell forever, love,
Don't let our parting grieve you.
I'll think of you in the cotton fields;
I'll pray for you when resting;
I'll look for you in every gang,
Like the bird that's lost her nesting.

Some songs had hidden, or encoded, messages. The lyrics to these tunes passed along information that had to be kept secret from slaveholders and overseers. For example, "Wade in the Water" told would-be fugitives that they should escape via the river. Among other reasons, the bloodhounds of the slave chasers would lose the scent at the water's edge. These song-messages became especially important to the slaves as stories of the Union army's whereabouts spread.

FREE AT LAST

With the end of the Civil War in April 1865 and the passage of the Thirteenth Amendment in December, the slaves' deepest longing became a reality. Slavery came to an official end in the United States.

Many former slaves began their lives as free people by going in search of family members who had escaped or been sold away. "You see after the war closed all the colored were looking round for their own folks," one former slave explained. "Husbands looking for their wives, and wives looking for their husbands, children looking for parents, parents looking for children, everything sure was scrambled up in those days."

For many people who had known nothing but an enslavement, liberation was frightening and confusing. A former slave from Tennessee later described the early days of freedom:

> I remember so well how the roads was full of folks walking and walking along when the [Negroes] were freed. Didn't know where they was going. Just going to see about something else somewhere else. Meet a body in the road and they asks, "Where you going?" "Don't know." "What you going to do?" "Don't know."

Some freed blacks, even during the war, moved onto properties deserted by whites who had fled the invading Union forces. The former slaves farmed the land and built their own dwellings, staking claims for ownership.

When news spread that the U.S. government intended to help freed people create homesteads, some African Americans welcomed the chance to acquire their own land. Others decided to stay with their former owners and work for wages. Ex-slave Frances Andrews explained it this way: "I heard about the 40 acres [16 ha] of land and a mule the ex-slaves would get after the war, but I didn't pay any attention to it. . . . I think this was just put out by the Yankees who didn't care about much 'cept getting money for themselves."

Despite such suspicions, some freed former slaves did receive parcels of land from the government. In addition, the Freedmen's Bureau—created by Congress just before the war ended—and numerous volunteer aid and relief societies sent teachers to the South, established schools and a handful of colleges, and provided medical attention for the freed people. At the same time, an increasing number of African Americans created their own all-black churches and schools, seeking the education they had been denied under slavery.

The early days after the war ended raised great hopes among the African Americans of the South. One former slave described the general feeling among the freed people. "We certainly were happy in those days . . . after the Surrender. We sung, we prayed, and we preached. You should of seen them [the freed slaves] shaking hands and hollering, 'Thank God my children can come with me to Church and no patterollers have to run after them.'"

MILES TO GO

True freedom, however, with all the rights and privileges guaranteed by the Constitution, would be a long time coming for African Americans. In many places in the South, laws would soon be enacted that were designed to keep African Americans segregated and in an inferior position. One writer for a Mississippi newspaper revealed the attitude of many former slaveholders: "The true station of the negro is that of a servant. The wants and state of our country demand that he should remain a servant."

Two years after the war, in August 1867, the Freedmen's Bureau issued a report detailing some of the abuses that freed African Americans endured:

The [black] freedmen were subjected to the punishments formerly inflicted upon slaves. Whipping, especially . . . was made the penalty for the most trifling misdemeanor. . . . [The freed people's] attempts at education provoked the most intense and bitter hostility . . . . In a single district, in a single month, forty-nine cases of violence, ranging from assault and battery to murder, in which whites were the aggressors and blacks the sufferers, were reported.

The legal abolition of slavery could not abolish hatred or racial prejudice. Even so, it was the indispensable first step toward justice and equality for the enslaved. Before the end of the 1800s, 350 years of African-American enslavement in the Americas would finally cease. The culture that the enslaved people carved out of hardship and sorrow to maintain their sense of humanity and community echoes into the present and enriches it.

Time Line

1492	The first free Africans arrive in Hispaniola with Christopher Columbus.
1502	Slavery is introduced in Hispaniola.
1550	The first slaves coming directly from Africa arrive in Brazil.
1619	Twenty Africans arrive in Jamestown, Virginia.
1672	Rice is first brought to South Carolina, eventually becoming a major cash crop dependent on slave labor.
1740s	South Carolinians develop indigo as a cash crop, leading to an increased dependency on slave labor.
1770s	Brazilian planters develop coffee plantations, leading to the importation of an additional 1.5 million slaves.
1770	Crispus Attucks dies in the "Boston Massacre" and is later proclaimed by the Patriots to be the first African American to die in the American Revolution.
1773	Phillis Wheatley becomes the first enslaved African-American woman to publish a book.
1775	African Americans fight for the Patriots in Revolutionary battles in Massachusetts. The royal governor of Virginia offers freedom to any slave who joins the British cause against the American Patriots.

1777	Vermont becomes a state and is the first state to abolish slavery.
1780	Pennsylvania enacts the first gradual emancipation law in the United States.
1783	Massachusetts outlaws slavery.
1793	The cotton gin is invented, resulting in the era of cotton plantations and the importation of more than 100,000 slaves.
1799	New York passes a law freeing the children of slaves born after July 4 of that year.
1800	Brazil becomes the nation with the largest slave population in the world.
1803	The Louisiana Purchase greatly expands U.S. territory, leading to the spread of slavery.
1807	George and Sophia Bell open the first school for African Americans in Washington, D.C.
1808	Congressional legislation ends the legal slave trade, but illegal trade continues until the Civil War.
1854	The Republican Party is formed with the intention of keeping slavery out of the Western territories.
1860	Abraham Lincoln is elected president.
1861	The Civil War begins.
1862	Slavery is abolished in Washington, D.C. Congress allows the enlistment of black soldiers.

1863	Lincoln signs the Emancipation Proclamation into law.
1865	Congress creates the Freedmen's Bureau to look after the needs of newly freed slaves throughout the South. The Civil War ends. Lincoln is assassinated. Congress approves the Thirteenth Amendment, abolishing slavery.

Glossary

abolitionist   A person who seeks an immediate end to slavery.

coffle   A group of chained slaves.

cotton gin   A machine developed in the 1790s to separate the seeds from the fiber of cotton. It led to mass production of cotton and a huge expansion of slavery in the United States.

Deep South   Usually refers to the part of the United States that includes Alabama, Arkansas, Florida, Georgia, Louisiana, Mississippi, Texas, and parts of the Carolinas and Tennessee.

emancipation   The act of freeing slaves.

fugitive   A person who escapes from slave owners or law officials.

indigo   A dark violet-blue or purple dye that was popular in Europe in the 1700s. Indigo was made from plants grown by slaves in South Carolina and Georgia.

insurrection   A rebellion or uprising.

Loyalist   An American who supported the British during the American Revolution.

maroons   Fugitive slaves who started their own communities in remote areas.

Parliament   Great Britain's lawmaking body.

Patriot   A person who supported freedom from Great Britain during the American Revolution.

plantation   A large farm that relied on slaves to produce one main crop.

prejudice   An unreasonable bias against or intolerance of others.

racism   Prejudice based on race.

secede   To break away from a larger group or government and become independent.

segregation   Separating whites and blacks and requiring them to use different public facilities, such as parks and schools.

Thirteenth Amendment   An amendment to the U.S. Constitution prohibiting slavery.

Further Reading

BOOKS

Cooper, Michael L. *Slave Spirituals and the Jubilee Singers.* New York: Clarion Books, 2001.

Diouf, Sylviane A. *Growing Up in Slavery.* New York: Millbrook Press, 2001.

Greene, Meg. *Slave Young, Slave Long: The American Slave Experience.* Minneapolis: Lerner Publications, 1999.

Hamilton, Virginia. *Her Stories: African American Folktales, Fairy Tales and True Tales.* New York: Blue Sky Press, 1996.

Paulsen, Gary. *Sarny: A Life Remembered.* New York: Delacorte, 1997.

WEB SITES

The African American Registry. "African American Dance, a History!" URL: http://www.aaregistry.com/african_american_history/749/African_American_Dance_a_history. Downloaded on September 7, 2005.

The Mariners' Museum—Captive Passage: The Transatlantic Slave Trade and the Making of the Americas. "Arrival: Life in the Americas—Slave Religion in Central and South America." URL: http://www.mariner.org/captivepassage/arrival/arr022.html. Downloaded on September 7, 2005.

Public Broadcasting Service (PBS). "Africans in America: Part 4, Narrative: Antebellum Slavery." URL: http://www.pbs.org/wgbh/aia/part4/4narr1.html. Downloaded on September 7, 2005.

Spartacus Educational. "Slave Families." URL: http://www.spartacus.schoolnet.co.uk/USASseparation.htm. Downloaded on September 7, 2005.

Index